Belongs
to
Tairne
Jackson

FRANCE

HISTORY AND
LANDSCAPE

FRANCE

HISTORY AND LANDSCAPE

EMMA HOWARD

COMPENDIUM

This 2008 edition published by

COMPENDIUM

© 2008 by Compendium Publishing Ltd.
43 Frith Street, Soho, London, W1D 4SA, UK

Design: Danny Gillespie
Color Reproduction: Anorax Imaging Ltd

ISBN: 978-1-905573-95-0

Printed and bound in China

PAGE 1: A familiar sight throughout the Côte
d'Azur are fields of lavender stretching to the
horizon. The temperate climate is perfect for
growing flowers all year round, and the nearby
town of Grasse has been the capital of the perfume
industry since the sixteenth century.

PAGES 2–3: La Rochelle in Poitou-Charentes is still
a vibrant seaport with an important history.
French settlers used this port to set off to a new
life in Montreal, Canada. It is known also as "the
white city" or "La Ville Blanche" because of the
bright limestone cliffs crowned with fourteenth
century towers, which often become luminous
when the sun's rays reflect back off them.

RIGHT: Honfleur is a pretty port on the
Normandy coast at the mouth of the Seine. In
medieval times its position gave it great strategic
importance, but in recent times it is better known
as the subject of many great artists.

CONTENTS

INTRODUCTION

A vast and surprisingly varied country, any visitor to France will be amazed by the numerous disparities in the traditions, people, landscape, and cultures across the nation. Long gone are the stereotypes of old—berets, stings of onions, and supposed insular arrogance. Each region of France has its own unique culture and this immense country encapsulates any landscape imaginable. From the pure sandy beaches of Biarritz in the southwest to the towering, wind-battered coastal cliffs of the Côte d'Opale on the north coast; the rolling plains of the Massif Central to the soaring snow-capped peak of Mont Blanc in the Alps, and not forgetting the vivacious, sophisticated capital city—Paris—also the comparatively tiny and quaint villages scattering the countryside trapped in their own little time warps where the worries of the western world never seem to find any foothold: France has something for everyone.

This is a country that wears its history proudly—like a badge of honor. Ruined castles attest to the hundred years of fighting the English; Roman ruins like those in Lyon and the Dordogne give us a glimpse into life under Roman occupation; and there is hardly a single town in France that does not have a memorial dedicated to the countless sons and fathers who were lost during the two world wars. Graveyards and shrines dedicated to the fallen soldiers of World War II are particularly prevalent along the northern coast of France, where Allied forces stormed in on June 4, 1944—the D-Day landings—and in the Picardy region where so many millions fell in the Great War. Some of the most poignant and heartbreaking examples lie in Normandy and Nord-Pas de Calais but perhaps the most shocking can be found further south in Limousin. The village of Oradour-sur-Glane had its entire population wiped out by German SS troops. The village has remained untouched since its populace was gunned down and the eerie quiet and emptiness only highlights what has been lost.

RIGHT: Standing in the centre of the world's biggest roundabout is the Arc de Triomphe. Commissioned by Napoleon to celebrate his numerous victories in battle, work began in 1806. Shortly afterward, Napoleon began losing and the arc remained incomplete. It was finally finished in 1836.

The huge variations in the language and cultures of France often surprises visitors, but when a country has been invaded as many times as France it is impossible for some of the idiosyncrasies of the occupiers not to be absorbed by the local inhabitants. Neighboring countries Germany, Spain, Italy, and England have all left their marks on the French people. In the far north, bordering Germany, the inhabitants of Alsace and Lorraine (both officially part of Germany until 1871) speak a dialect of German, and the architecture is profoundly Germanic with half-timber ed chalet-style houses filling every village. The proximity of Spain to the regions of Provence and Languedoc-Roussillon has stamped a definite Spanish feel on the area. Colorful buildings line the coasts and cities in a style reminiscent of colonial Spain, and the people cling tightly to their Catalonian roots and language. It is still one of the few places in France where bull-fighting is sill in practice.

Even as far north as Brittany the differences are still marked: this department fiercely defends its Celtic roots.

The dress, traditions, music, and festivals still strongly reflect the Celtic origins of the region.

Of course, France is most famous for its beautifully preserved buildings, some dating as far back as the Middle Ages or beyond. Many of the major towns and cities have imposing twelfth or thirteenth century twin-towered cathedrals, echoing the primary Notre-Dame Cathedral in Paris. Some even manage to outshine the splendor of their Parisian cousin—for example the Notre Dame in Amiens is twice the size of its Parisian counterpart.

Hundreds of chateaux, each holding their own particular place in history, spread across the landscape. Some of the best sit in the Loire Valley, the valley of kings. It was here that many nobles built their sprawling mansion homes and some glorious examples still remain. The Chateau de Chambord sitting in its own national park is the definitive French chateau. It tool more than 1,800 artists and workers more than fifteen years just to decorate, yet King Francois I, who commissioned its construction

only stayed there a total of forty-two days. Yet there is also the majestic Chateau at Versailles, the building of which almost bankrupted the country and its ostentatious opulence led to an open revolution and the Republic.

One of the proudest parts of French culture is its enjoyment of all things relating to food and drink. Much of the country is filled with vineyards. Each region has its own specialty wine and food, including cheese, pastries, and delicacies such as truffles. World-renowned cheeses and wines were discovered here and still made to age-old recipes. Camembert is the domain of Normandy; Roquefort is made from thousand of gallons of ewes' milk in Languedoc-Roussillon; and of course, the Champagne region is identified for one very important export. Périgord in Aquitaine is split into four parts, two relating to food—purple Périgord because of the color of its grapes; black Périgord due to the abundance of truffles (called black gold by the locals) in the area. White and green Périgord refer to the limestone rocks and the lush landscape.)

This book attempts to capture some of the beauty of France with its fascinating history and stunning landscapes by following a circular "tour de France," traveling around the regions, starting on the northeastern borders in Lorraine-Alsace. From there, we travel westward toward Brittany, down the south coast to Aquitaine, where France and Spain meet. then back up toward the center and the regions lying on the eastern borders alongside Italy and Switzerland.

BELOW: High on a plateau sits the scenic village of Monestier du Percy. Situated in the Isère department just 35 miles from Grenoble, this untouched town basks in the surrounding countryside, protected by the encircling mountains.

ALSACE AND LORRAINE

BELOW: The covered bridges (or Ponts Couverts) in Strasbourg once formed part of a massive defensive system around the city. From here, soldiers were safe from enemy missiles and occasionally the towers would be used as a prison.

ALSACE AND LORRAINE

These two regions of far northeastern France are found nestled comfortably between the Vosges Mountains and the River Rhine. Being so close to the German border has inevitably influenced the culture, architecture, and even the language of the area. The local inhabitants speak Alsatian (or Elsassich) an Alemannic dialect of German.

France's smallest province, Alsace, is famed for its rolling pastoral hills and breathtaking beauty. Its capital, Strasbourg, is an idiosyncratic mixture of modern office buildings and conference centers along its outskirts and the gorgeous nineteenth century mansions and half-timbered houses that can be found in Strasbourg old-town—its cosmopolitan center. Strasbourg is also famed for its supremely Gothic fifteenth century cathedral, Cathédrale

Notre Dame, and the huge Palais de l'Europe which houses the European Parliament and the European Court of Human Rights.

One of the most popular enticements into Alsace is the famed "Route du Vin." This 110-mile road starts in the walled city of Molsheim then winds in and out of various charming villages where one can savor the traditional Alsatian food and locally made wines. Alsace is prized for its dry white wine, which smells misleadingly sweet. Amongst the most recognized are Riesling, Tokay d'Alsace, and Gewurztraminer. When touring the Route du Vin travelers will often be served these wines with the traditional accompanying dishes, such as choucroute (a kind of pickled cabbage served with meat), foie gras, or a sweet cheese pie.

Alsace is also well-known for its stork population: the stork's nest is one of the region's most loved symbols. In the past storks used to nest on chimneys or on cart-wheels hoisted up onto poles but in the late 1980s the stork population went into rapid decline. Thus began the Stork Reintroduction Center based in the Chateau de Kintzheim, which also takes care of many other species of birds. It is possible to see eagles, vultures, and even condors swooping around the ruined castle battlements.

Lorraine has a less salubrious reputation than its neighbor as some of the major towns are seen as being too industrial and overdeveloped. However, it does still boast several picturesque prairies and forests, and its two principal towns have been undergoing something of a restoration of late. Lorraine's capital city, Metz, can lay claim to housing the largest art-glass windows in the world in its Cathédrale St.-Étienne, and in the old town is the oldest church in France, St. Pierre aux Normains, which dates back to the fourth century. Much of Lorraine's history, however, lies in the ancient city of Nancy, the old seat of the Duke of Lorraine. This cultured and striking location has a wealth of attractions in its center—from the Musée des Beaux-Arts, which houses an enormous collection of Art-Nouveau paintings and glass work, to the Palais Ducal, an impressive residence that contains the Musée Historique Lorraine.

In the past the proximity of the German border has had more disastrous consequences. Evidence of this can be seen in the numerous war memorials scattered in this area, the most famous being the battlefield at Verdun where an estimated 800,000 people died. Walking around the remains of the forts and trenches is a poignant reminder of how many lost their lives.

BELOW: Looking at the peaceful and quaint village of Kayersberg, it is hard to believe that it has suffered a rather violent history. Due to its strategic importance—it sits at the entrance to the Weiss valley—a fortress was built around the town in 1227. Keyersberg was at the center of many battles between European ruling houses. Today it is thought to be one of the most beautiful villages in France.

PREVIOUS PAGE: The beautiful village of Hunawihr is encircled by vineyards and rolling pastures. This village is surrounded by a hexagonal wall and houses a sixteenth-century church, which is both Catholic and Protestant.

ABOVE: During World War I, the village of Douaumont in the Verdun battlefields was utterly destroyed in a barrage of constant artillery. The village was never rebuilt and all that remains is a battle-scarred field and a few rusty artillery shells.

RIGHT: Colmar, the capital of the Haut-Rhine department, is a colorful Alsatian town full of wooden buildings backing onto winding rivers and cobbled streets.

PREVIOUS PAGE: Sitting on the Moselle River is the capital of Lorraine—Metz. Many of the town's most impressive buildings date from when Metz was part of the German empire. Perhaps the best of these is the Cathédrale St. Etienne, the thirteenth-century construction famed for its art-glass windows.

RIGHT: The town hall in the walled village of Turckheim, Alsace. This medieval village still employs a nightwatchman, who stops on each corner to announce whether all is well.

PAGE 22–23: The pretty town of Breitenbach sits in the protective arc of the Vosges mountains. The mountains are full of dense forests, lakes, and undulating pastures, making it an ideal hiking spot.

LEFT: Right on the edge of the German border, the pretty town of Wissembourg is typically Alsace. Meaning "white castle," Wissembourg is a quiet town most of the year—until Pentecost when the streets fill with folk music and festivals. It is also the birthplace of Marie Lescynca, who went on to marry Louis XV and become queen.

ABOVE: A small lane in the village of Eguisheim in Alsace. The name means home of Egino and can be dated back as far as 720 A.D. In the center of the village are the remains of a thirteenth-century fortified castle. The village was also once home to Bruno of Eguisheim, later to become Pope Léon IX.

PAGE 28: One of the many timbered houses in the beautiful village of Kayersberg. The houses are traditionally covered in geraniums during the summer, decorating the whole village in a bloom of color.

PAGE 29: The twin churches of Saint Peter and Saint Paul in Rosheim were built in the twelfth century and are a triumph of the Romanesque style. It is also the second-largest church in Alsace and boast magnificent art-glass windows.

LEFT: The Verdun Ossuary contains the remains of
130,000 fallen soldiers, both French and German,
who are buried in mass graves and have never been
identified. A nearby museum recreates the
appalling conditions endured by the men during
the Battle of Verdun, which lasted 300 days.

ABOVE: Half way between Strasbourg and
Mulhouse, Ribeauvillé is an attractive town with
5,000 inhabitants.

31

LEFT: In 1949, Strasbourg was chosen to be the site of the Council of Europe, and since 1979, it has been a seat of the European Parliament. In fact most business takes place in Brussels and Strasbourg sees sessions on only four days each month. This building—the Immeuble Louise Weiss (also known as IPE IV)—has the largest parliamentary assembly room in Europe and of any democratic institution in the world.

CHAMPAGNE AND ARDENNES

CHAMPAGNE AND ARDENNES

Though covered in dense forests, rolling hills striped with vineyards, quaint delightful villages, and the impressive valley of the River Meuse, this region is world renowned for one thing in particular—that light sparkling white wine so affiliated with luxury and expense, Champagne. A Benedictine monk named Dom Perignon accidentally invented champagne in the seventeenth century. It is reported that his first words on discovering his new creation were "Come quickly I am seeing stars!" Nowadays this region produces millions of gallons of champagne each year and only vintners operating in this area are allowed to use that prestigious name. Some of the most impressive sights available to visitors are the underground caverns and cellars where the finished bottles are allowed to cool. Under the town of Épinay there are sixty miles of underground grottos to explore. In the Lanson labyrinths ornate statues are carved into the walls, and the Piper-Heidseck cellar has a small subterranean train to convey visitors through its vast hollows.

The most historically significant city in the province is Reims, the coronation city where twenty-six kings have been crowned in the imposing gothic Cathédrale Notre Dame. Clovis, the first king of the Franks, was baptized here in 496 A.D. Although a little care-worn today, the western façade of the cathedral still boasts some spectacular thirteenth-century carvings including the Smiling Angel situated on the north doorway. It is also famed for its stunning art-glass windows. The celebrated Rose Window ates from the thirteenth century but there are also more recent additions, such as some twentieth century glasswork designed by Chagall.

A little way south of Reims is the large town of Épernay, the true wine lovers' capital. The Möet and Chandon firm is based here, and nearby Hautvilliers is the birthplace of Dom Perignon.

Located a little further south is the beautiful city of Troyes. Still reminiscent of the Renaissance era, the town has kept much of its old-world charm. Half-timbered

houses line the narrow streets, and nine magnificent churches hold many religious treasures and supreme examples old art-glass that rival those seen in any of the main French cathedrals. Not far from here is the Cross of Lorraine, a giant pink granite monument to the memory of France's favorite hero, Charles de Gaulle. It is in the local village of Colombey-les-Deux-Eglises that de Gaulle had his country retreat. His house, called La Boisserie, now houses a museum, full of intriguing de Gaulle memorabilia.

When traveling into the Ardennes the rugged beauty of the region is immediately apparent, with most of the area carpeted in thick forest and steep hills. Striking though it is, the difficult terrain of the area has made agriculture problematical, and many inhabitants leave the Ardennes each year. In fact the population has been decreasing steadily since 1982 and it is now one of France's most sparsely populated areas. The region is rich on minerals, especially iron ore. Many of the iron works are open for tours, and locals parks have an abundance of wrought-iron artwork. It was through the Ardennes hills that Germany first invaded France during World War II. It had been considered improbable that any significant sized army would be able to find passage over the steep hills,

unfortunately for France this was not the case and once in enemy territory the German army marched easily into Paris.

PREVIOUS PAGE: Interior view of side nave and art-glass window in Reims Cathedral.

LEFT: Local champagne producers are immensely proud of the name "Champagne," and display it proudly. All over the region signs like this are displayed like badges of honor. In the same way, they fiercely defend it against any interlopers who would dare use it undeservedly.

ABOVE: The Bollinger Magnums cave. Bottles are stored and aged here for at least ten years before they are considered mature enough to be tasted by the public.

PREVIOUS PAGE: Outside the Laurent-Perrier Champagne house in Tours-Sur-Marne sits this charming fountain, advising all passers-by to "never drink water." After all, when in Champagne country, why drink anything else?

ABOVE: The main portal of the Cathédrale Notre Dame in Reims is dedicated to the Virgin Mary with the surrounding statuary telling her story. Above the portal is a rose window and then above that is the gallery of Kings. A statue of Clovis, the first King of France, stands in the center with his successors around him.

RIGHT: Ornate sculptures have been carved into the underlying limestone in the Pommery cellars, Each champagne house adds its own touch of glamor or luxury to its caves.

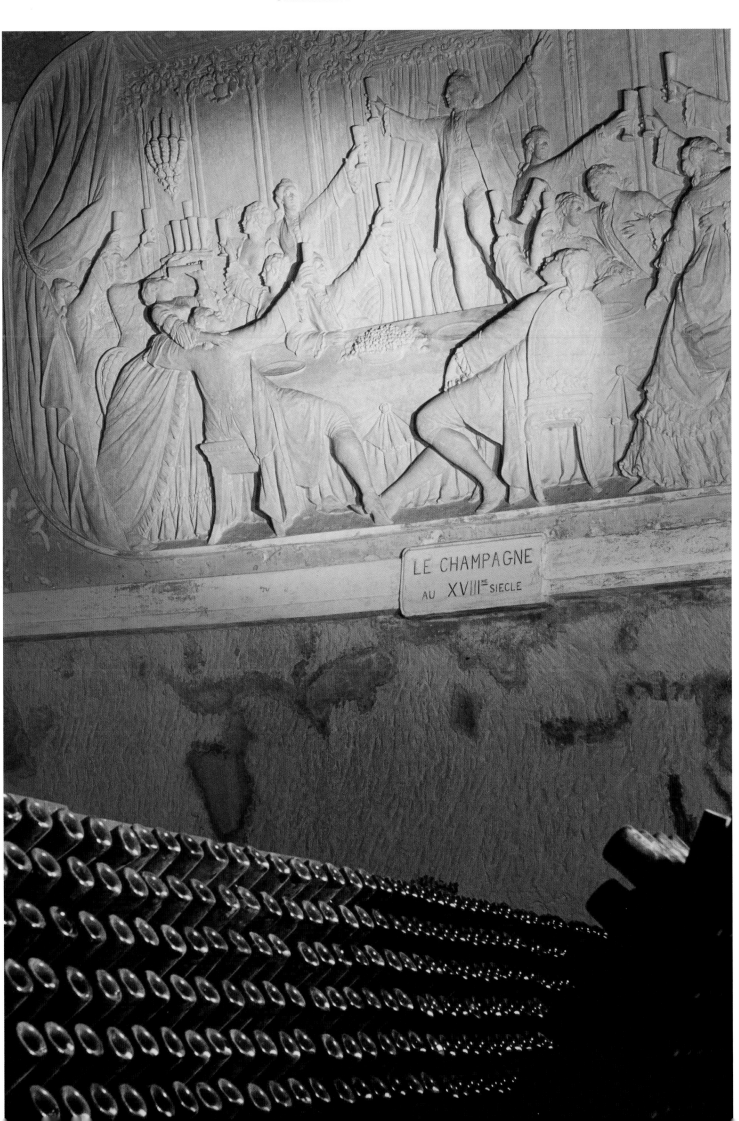

LE CHAMPAGNE
AU XVIIIᵐᵉ SIÈCLE

PREVIOUS PAGE: Surrounding the town of Épinay are countless vineyards. This is not surprising as Épinay is considered by wine lovers as the genuine heart of the Champagne region. Some of the most prestigious Champagne houses have made their home here.

ABOVE: The lush, verdant forests of the Ardennes are home to a cornucopia of wild animals. For this reason one of the most popular past-times here is hunting. The chasse (or hunt) is extremely popular throughout France but the Ardennes attracts tourists specifically for this reason.

ABOVE RIGHT: By following the sign for the Route du Champagne, connoisseurs will be guided from one Champagne house to another where they will be able to sample the local wares.

RIGHT: This quaint and rather small archway belies the vast labyrinth of catacombs that lie beneath the Bollinger Champagne house.

PREVIOUS PAGE: All over this region, the gently sloping hills are striped with rows of vines as far as the eye can see. In the tiny rural village of Chamery alone, there are four Champagne Houses.

ABOVE: Close to the Belgian border, near the Ardennes hills is the town of Charlesville-Mézieres. In the centre is the magnificent Place Ducal, a larger version of the Place des Vosges in Paris. At its centre stands a monument to Charles de Gonzague, the seventeenth century duke who decided to have the city built on his twenty-sixth birthday.

RIGHT: This charming French village is Hautvilliers, the birth place of Dom Perignon, the seventeenth century inventor of Champagne. He both lived and worked in the nearby abbey and it is thanks to him that the Champagne region of France is such a household name today.

BELOW: Located near Reims, the Champagne Pommery Estate is an impressive Tudor style building above ground. Visitors are encouraged to descend a steep staircase, approximately 116 steps downwards, to tour the caves, learn about the process of making Champagne and of course to sample the finished product.

52

LEFT: A rear view of the Cathédrale Notre Dame in Reims. The thirteenth century cathedral is situated right next to the Palais du Tau, which used to be the royal residence when the crowned heads of France stayed in Reims. Nowadays it is a museum housing several precious items and tapestries.

BELOW LEFT: Throughout France there are countless historical or archaeological treasures to be found. Here, near the church of St Remi in Reims is a Roman Triumphal Arch dating from the third century.

RIGHT: This interior view of the renowned Rose Window in the Cathédrale Notre Dame in Reims highlights not only the magnificence of the glass windows but also shows the contrasting simplicity of the surrounding nave, thus making the stained glass all the more striking.

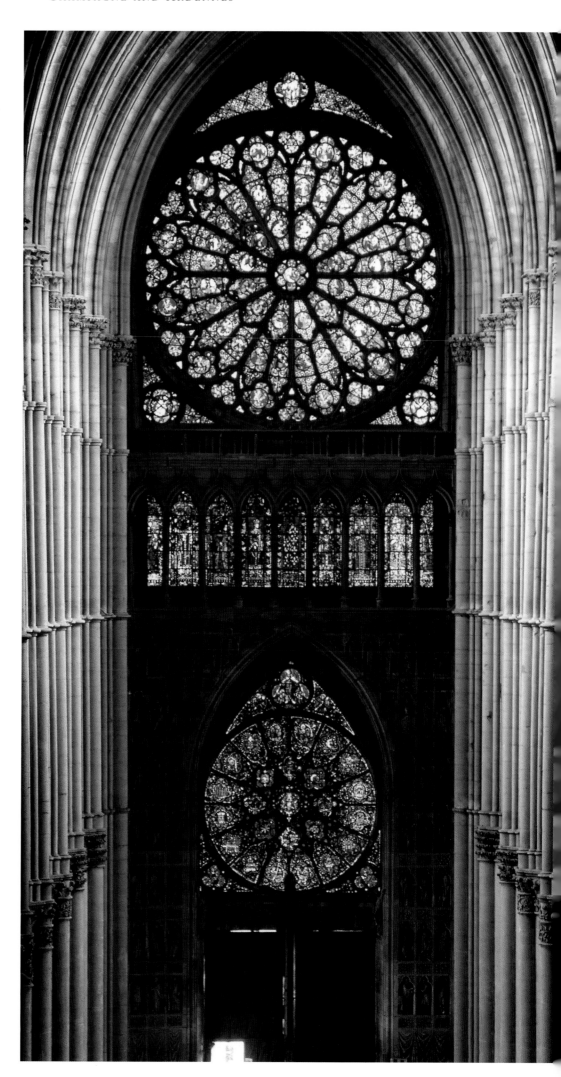

PREVIOUS PAGE: A forest of Poplar trees stand to attention in the late evening sun. Only in France are trees uniformly planted in this manner and it is a stark contrast to the rest of Ardennes natural yet beautiful wilderness.

RIGHT: Towering over the surrounding countryside, the Lorraine Cross is a striking memorial to France's favorite son, Charles de Gaulle. Near the village of Colombey-les-Deux-Eglises, the cross stands at 142 feet and is made of Clarte pink granite.

NORD-PAS DE CALAIS
AND PICARDY

NORD-PAS DE CALAIS AND PICARDY

War has taken a heavy toll on this, the northernmost corner of France. Charles De Gaulle once refered to Nord-Pas de Calais as a "fatal avenue" due to its strategic importance and the numerous invading armies that have marched through here on their way to conquer more of the country.

During the Roman occupation, in the fourth and fifth centuries A.D., Germanic tribes were hired to defend the borders between Boulogne and Cologne. This led to many of the inhabitants north of Lille speaking a form of Middle Dutch, a linguistic diversity that is evident to this day.

Throughout the Middle Ages, Calais was owned by the English while the rest of the country was split between Flanders, Boulogne, and even the Holy Roman Empire. It took the mighty House of Burgundy to reunite all the territory—excepting Calais—in the fifteenth century along with much of Belgium. It was not until 1697 and the reign of Louis XIV that the whole of Nord-Pas de Calais became a part of France completely.

In the nineteenth century the region embraced the industrial age and became one of the leading centers for commerce, second only to Alsace. When Alsace-Lorraine was captured by Germany during the Franco-Prussian War of 1870, Nord-Pas de Calais became the primary center of France's industry—that is until the dawning of World War I. Once again, its strategically important position was to be its downfall.

Occupied by Germany for much of the war, hundreds of miles of land and countless villages were utterly devastated during four years of trench warfare. Nord-Pas de Calais endured more destruction than any other region of France. It had barely managed to get on its feet again when World War II began and Germany took possession once more. The German forces used the area as a launch site at first for Luftwaffe attacks and later for the V-1 flying bombs. Because of this Nord-Pas de Calais was bombarded by Allied bombs and artillery.

Liberated in the main by September 1944, pockets of German forces resisted for longer and only surrendered toward the very end of the war; indeed, Dunkirk was the last French town to be set free—on May 9, 1945. Unsurprizingly, memorials and graveyards scatter the area, including the mesmerizing Vimy Memorial—Canada's superlative tribute to its lost soldiers in the Great War.

Since then the region has suffered a slump in fortunes due to the closure of many coal mines and steel mills which were the backbone of its economy. Fortunately, the opening of the Channel Tunnel and the Eurostar has meant that tourism has boosted prosperity in the area and given it a new lease of life.

Like Nord-Pas de Calais, Picardy also suffered greatly during the war, with most of its capital, Reims, being razed to the ground. Though it once enjoyed a reputation as being a flourishing textile-making city, there is little evidence to show for this today. The only surviving major monument is the Cathédrale Notre Dame. The largest of its kind in the country, this grand edifice is twice the size of the Notre Dame in Paris.

The landscape of Picardy has managed to recover from the ravages of trench-warfare very well and nowadays people will traval for miles to see the rolling poppy fields where once so many men fought and died for freedom.

PREVIOUS PAGE: Surrounded by dense forests, the Chateau de Compiègne was an ideal hunting retreat for royalty. Built in 1374 for Charles V, it has been modified many times. Even after the departure of the monarchy Napoleon III and his wife, Eugenie, used it as an autumn residence and redecorated in Second Empire style.

LEFT: A country so torn apart by war looks to the Divine in all aspects of life. Here, even the farmers have a religious icon in the midst of their harvest.

ABOVE: The spectacular view from the top of the northern tower in Amiens Cathedral overlooking the city.

PAGE 62–63: Once called "the oldest new building in France," the medieval-styled Chateau Pierrefonds in Picardy was actually built in the nineteenth century and used by Napoleon III as a hunting retreat.

RIGHT: Separating Old Lille from New Lille, the Place du General de Gaulle is a convivial square lined with cafés and restaurants—the ideal place to sit back and enjoy a part of the famous French café culture.

PAGE 66: This haunting sculpture is part of the Vimy War Memorial. This site is dedicated to all those Canadian soldiers who died during battles that took place here.

PAGE 67: One of the many war memorials scattered across this region.

LEFT: The immense Notre Dame Cathedral—seen here towering over the River Somme—in Amiens is 575 feet long and was built in 1220 to accommodate the head of St. John the Baptist.

ABOVE: The interior of the eastern nave in the cavernous cathedral in Amiens. Built by Robert de Luzarches and eventually completed in 1238, the Gothic monument is the largest of its kind in France.

PAGE 70–71: Known as the Cote d'Opale because of the glistening green and blue hues of the sea, the twenty-five miles of coastline between Calais and Boulogne is often buffeted by storms and gale-force winds.

PAGE 72–73: A view of the lush green landscape on the approach to the Côte d'Opale. Seeing the contrasting green of the land and the shining blue sea, it is easy to see why early settlers equated it to the shimmering surface of an opal.

LEFT: The Chateau de Chantilly was built in two parts: the first part was a mansion built in 1528 that was destroyed during the French Revolution. Since then it has been rebuilt as the Grand Château in the 1870s. The smaller section or the Petit Château was constructed in the 1560s for Anne de Montmorency, one of the powerful Montmorency family, one of the oldest and most illustrious families in France.

PAGE 76: Many of the houses in and around the centre of Lille have been lovingly restored back to their former glory. Here it is possible to see the ornate details on the eighteenth century town house.

PAGE 77: Lille's Chamber of Commerce in the central square was built in a neo-Flemish design and has a belfry 250-feet high. It is now a center for many cultural occasions such as art exhibitions and also conferences.

ABOVE: The trenches at Vimy have been reinforced and kept as a reminder of the harsh and cramped conditions endured by the soldiers who lived and died here.

ABOVE RIGHT: The old Chateau de Fere in Tardenois, Picardy, was built in the thirteenth century. Very little remains of the chateau itself, just a few ruins on a hillside, but the galleried bridge is still an impressive sight. King Louis XIII confiscated the castle after the death of Henri II, the last Duke of Montmerency and it was soon demolished.

BELOW RIGHT: Just north from Amiens is the sleepy town of Montreuil. This quiet place sits on a hill and is surrounded by a medieval citadel and its bastions. Inside the gate, the town is full of cobbled streets and half-timbered houses.

RIGHT: The Saint-Leu Quarter of Amiens was once the heart of its booming textile industry, but after sixty percent of the city was destroyed in the war, very little remained. After intense restoration, this area is now the hip place to be. Cobbled streets and cottages run alongside a maze of canals which make it one of the best places in the city to relax with a coffee and enjoy the atmosphere.

PAGE 82: The Grand Place in Lille is the central meeting point for many visitors and locals alike. Surrounded by perfectly restored eighteenth and nineteenth century houses and filled with pleasant cafés, the town enjoys a reputation of being one of the friendliest in France.

PAGE 83: The Channel Tunnel from Dover, England to Calais, France was a costly undertaking. It has certainly made a difference to passengers who can now enjoy first-class service between Brussels or Paris and London in under three hours by Eurostar train.

NORMANDY

NORMANDY

Normandy has had its fair share of invaders and battles. From the Vikings in the ninth century through to William the Conqueror in 1066 and finally the D-Day landings in 1944, history has left an indelible mark on the landscape. The area is strewn with fortified castles and many of the smaller towns were permanently destroyed during the 1944 Battle of Normandy. However there is much more to the area than memorials and monuments. Nowadays this area is famed for its cheese, its cider and cider brandy (calvados), and the undeniable beauty of its countryside. While still honoring the old, Normandy has embraced the new.

The stylish city of Rouen is a perfect example of Normandy's robust spirit. Originally built on the Roman city of Rotomagus, Rouen has suffered through many difficult times. The city was destroyed by fire and ravaged by plague during the Middle Ages. Occupied by the English during the Hundred Years War, it was here that Joan of Arc was tried and then burned at the stake for heresy in 1431. Now magnificently restored after the damage of World War II, it is a bustling cosmopolitan city with a perfectly renovated medieval quarter at its heart.

Other towns have not been so faithfully restored. Take Le Havre. Completely razed during the bombings of World War II, it was rebuilt under the careful eye of Auguste Perret, a Belgian architect who seemed to have an unfathomable love of concrete. This much more modern-looking town is now listed as a World Heritage Site by UNESCO.

Perhaps one of the best-known sights in all of Normandy is Mont Saint Michel, founded in the eighth century by Aubert, the Bishop of Arrandes, after he was reportedly visited by Archangel Michael. Even now a statue of the angel stands astride the abbey roof, watching over all those beneath him. According to local folklore, Mont Saint Michel is also one of the tombs of the sea where lost souls travel in order to find peace. In 966 A.D., Richard I, the Duke of Normandy made a gift of the island to the

Benedictines. By the eleventh century it resembled less of an abbey and more of a military fortress. In fact, during the Hundred Years War, Mont St. Michel was the only part of Northern France that withstood all English assaults and never once fell into enemy hands. Finally in 1966 the Benedictines had their island restored to them and now the entire island is a UNESCO World Heritage Site.

Normandy is also commonly known as "Camembert Country" and while traveling cross its green pastures it is impossible not to notice the huge number of cows grazing out on the fields. When considering how much Camembert is made here it is not surprising that cows outnumber people. Between 10,000 and 15,000 tonnes of Camembert is made in Normandy each year and it is even regulated by the same governing body that controls the makers of vintage French wine.

PREVIOUS PAGES: The countryside of Normandy—lush, green, and filled with cattle. Legend has it that the inventor of Camembert, Marie Herel, was given the recipe by an abbot from Brie who was fleeing the Revolutionaries.

LEFT: Normandy is the home of French cider and this quaint little shop in the coastal town of Honfleur offers the usual Normandy fare of cider or Calvados. Perfect with a wedge of Camembert!

ABOVE: This is the Rue du Gros Horloge in Rouen. The recently restored street is framed by a gatehouse from the sixteenth century and the large one-handed medieval clock is the Gros Horloge of the street's title. Gustave Flaubert, the author of *Madame Bovary*, was born and based his famous novel here in Rouen.

PREVIOUS PAGES: The Basilica of Sainte Therese in Lisieux houses many relics of the popular saint, nicknamed the "Little Flower."

ABOVE: The Abbaye aux Hommes in Caen was built by William the Conqueror just after he was excommunicated from the Catholic Church for marrying Matilda of Flanders, his cousin. This eventually came to be William's final resting place although his remains never found peace here. His tomb was destroyed in the sixteenth century and again in the eighteenth century so now the only vestige of William is a single thigh bone.

RIGHT: This statue of Joan of Arc stands in the Place du Vieux Marché in Rouen. This is the same square in which the nineteen-year old saint was burnt at the stake for heresy in 1431.

PREVIOUS PAGES: Known as Falaise d'Aval, this imposing headland is located near the pretty coastal town of Étretat. The French writer Maupassant once equated this towering arch in the chalk cliffs to an elephant dipping its trunk in the water.

RIGHT: Perhaps one of the best-known sights in all of France, Mont St. Michel is a beautifully preserved medieval monument. The lofty spires and turrets of the abbey have fared well despite a tumultuous history, and even the sea has taken little toll. In fact the shores around the island are notorious for their fierce tides. The difference between high and low tide can be anything up to fifty feet and the island itself can go from being surrounded by miles of calm sandy beaches to completely submerged in water in less than six hours.

PAGE 96–97: Normandy has a wealth of ancient chateaux and manor houses, of which the Chateau de Saint Germain-de-Livet in Lisieux is a marvelous example. This gorgeous sixteenth century building is enveloped in the rolling Normandy countryside, decorated with sixteenth century frescos, and surrounded by stunning landscaped gardens.

WoW!!

Isn't that beautiful?

LEFT: Immediately recognizable to anyone who has seen his paintings, this was the home of Claude Monet from 1883 until his death in 1926 at 85. He worked tirelessly and his garden was his biggest inspiration. Giverny now houses a Claude Monet museum and visitors can tour the gardens that have now become so associated with Monet's most famous works.

RIGHT: The flame monument at Sword Beach commemorates the landing of French Forces during World War II.

LEFT: The ruins of the twelfth century Chateau Gaillard are located in Les Andelys, a small town on the Seine southeast of Rouen. Built in 1196, this chateau protected the English territories in Normandy until King Henry IV had it torn down in 1403.

PREVIOUS PAGES: The riverside town of Les Andelys sits on the convergence of the River Seine and the River Gambon. The ruins of Richard the Lionheart's castle lie close by.

LEFT: Another view of the peaceful town of Les Andelys. It boasts some of the finest and panoramic views of the River Seine winding it way through the countryside.

PAGE 106: Another view of Mont St. Michel. Looking closely, one is able to make out the statue of the Archangel Michael, fighting a dragon symbolizing the constant struggle between good and evil.

PAGE 107: The charming coastal town of Honfleur has an illustrious history. The heart of the town is the old port, named the Vieux Basin. The explorer Samuel de Champlain set sail from Honfleur on his way to establish Quebec. In 1681 another adventurer, Cavelier de la Salle, set off from this point to explore America. He later named the town he founded Louisiana after King Louis XIV. These fine wooden houses once looked out over the sea but, due to silt deposits from the Seine blocking the waterfront, they are now several hundred feet inland.

LEFT: The Vire Valley stretches out over endless rolling hills and pastures. Normandy is one of the greenest and most fertile regions in all of France.

ABOVE: Viewed through Rouen's delightful Old Town is the Église St.-Ouen, a magnificent fourteenth-century gothic abbey.

BRITTANY

BELOW: Here at the land's end is the Côte de Granit Rose, named after the rosy-colored stones in this area. The further west one goes in Brittany, the more untamed and tempestuous the landscape becomes.

BRITTANY

Fiercely proud of their independent heritage and separated from the rest of France by dense forests, Brittany has always been a province apart. Originally peopled by migrating Celts in the sixth century B.C. who brought their customs and religion to the area, their legacy remains even to this day.

During the ninth century A.D., after the departure of the Romans, a Breton warrior named Nominoë led a revolt a against French rule. The result was the independent Duchy of Brittany. Unfortunately, being positioned between two opposing and much greater kingdoms, France and England, put the new duchy in a precarious position. To ensure its safety a number of tactical royal weddings took place until finally, in 1532, Brittany was reunited with its motherland.

Today, Brittany still retains its sense of exclusivity and the locals consider themselves Celtic first and French second. In fact, the local traditional dress and music bears more than a passing resemblance to those in both Welsh and Scottish customs. The local Breton bonnet is similar, although much taller, than its Welsh cousin and music is played on a "biniou," an instrument very similar to a set of Scottish bagpipes.

Brittany encapsulates the départements of Finistère, the Côtes d'Armor where the shallow sea level creates a bay of such intense green hues that it has been named Cote d'Émeraude (the Emerald Coast), Ille-et-Vilaine, Loire-Atlantique, and Morbihan. To the west of Brittany's coast is the famed Côte de Granit Rose. Here the mild pink tones of the granite reflect the light of the morning or evening sun to create a spectacular orange vista.

This region also possesses many megalithic monuments. Near the small town of Carnac there are over three thousand dolmens and menhirs standing in ancient circles. Many visitors have speculated about the purpose of these stones but local villagers remain disinclined to discuss the subject. As well as mysterious stone circles, Brittany is also well-known for its calvaries, ornately sculpted carvings depicting the crucifixion, which can be found throughout the region.

The walled city of St. Malo is a well-known site in this area and is now popular with tourists. This twelfth century fortified town was an important port in the seventeenth and eighteenth centuries during hostilities between France and England. Nowadays it welcomes many visitors onto its ramparts—English or otherwise. Originally an island it later became joined to the mainland by a sand peninsula in the thirteenth century.

LEFT: One of the most peculiar sights of the Brittany coast is the famous house built between two enormous rocks. This tiny cottage is protected from all storms, perhaps even hurricanes, by its two immense and constant sentries.

RIGHT: The gently undulating coastline of the Côte de Granit Rose is a perfect place for otters to thrive. Here at the Pointe du Chateau, local marine wildlife has flourished and on the nearby offshore islands, there are more than 20,000 marine birds, including puffins, fulmars, and razorbills.

PAGE 114–115: During the late nineteenth century the small picturesque village of Pont Aven became a huge inspiration for the painter Paul Gaugin. His famous painting "The Yellow Christ" was completed here and the small Musée d'Orsay in the village center has the yellow crucifix which inspired his work.

Beautiful

PAGE 116: The perfectly preserved medieval town of Vitré is one of the best Brittany has to offer. Old timber-framed houses nestle under the protective spires of the town's immense castle.

PAGE 117: A closer look at the beautiful medieval settlement of Dinan. Here, in the heart of the old town, is the Tour de l'Horloge, where it is possible to climb the tower onto a small balcony and enjoy a spectacular view.

Pretty

LEFT: St. Malo Harbor is home to tall ships and yachts. Known for its rapidly changing tides and inclement weather, St. Malo can be covered in threatening stormy skies one minute then azure skies pierce the clouds and the sun is shining in the next.

PAGE 120–121: Louet Island, just off Morlaix Bay in the northeastern Finistère region of Brittany. Brittany's coastline is peppered with charming islands and taking a boat is the best way to view them all.

LEFT: One of the many lighthouses along the coast of Brittany. This lighthouse in Pointe du Raz at Cape Sizun is just visible in the distance against the dusky orange sky.

ABOVE: This peaceful view of Nantes across a blossoming field of sunflowers belies the town's turbulent past. Although not officially classed as part of Brittany, it was the capital of the region until 1972. Now classed under the Loire-Atlantique, Nantes clings tightly to its Breton roots and no amount of government meddling will stop Nantes remaining Breton in its heart.

PAGE 124–125: Brittany's capital of Rennes is a vibrant university city with many impressive buildings. This is the Palais St. George and its formal gardens. Much of Rennes was burned down in 1720 when fire gutted the entire city, as a result most of the main edifices date from this time.

RIGHT: Frozen in time, the small town of Dinan with its cobbled streets and bowed timber houses is a slice of medieval history. Hundreds of thousands of visitors flock to this town every year to enjoy the Fête des Ramparts when locals dress up in historic costumes.

PAGE 128–129: The coastline of Northern Brittany is scattered with old lighthouses. These were extremely important for the ships maneuvering around the rocky outcrops that run the length of this often treacherous coastline.

LEFT: The thirteenth-century gothic Cathédrale St. Pierre in the walled old town of Vannes is only accessible through a maze of winding alleyways.

ABOVE: Vannes has always played an important role in Breton history. During Brittany's revolt against France, it was Vannes that the hero Nominoë named the capital of the Duchy of Brittany in the ninth century. Later on, when the province reunited with France, the announcement was made here in Vannes.

PAGE 132–133: The coastal town of Brest was mostly destroyed during World War II but its thirteenth-century castle managed to survive. The port is still a busy harbor and naval base.

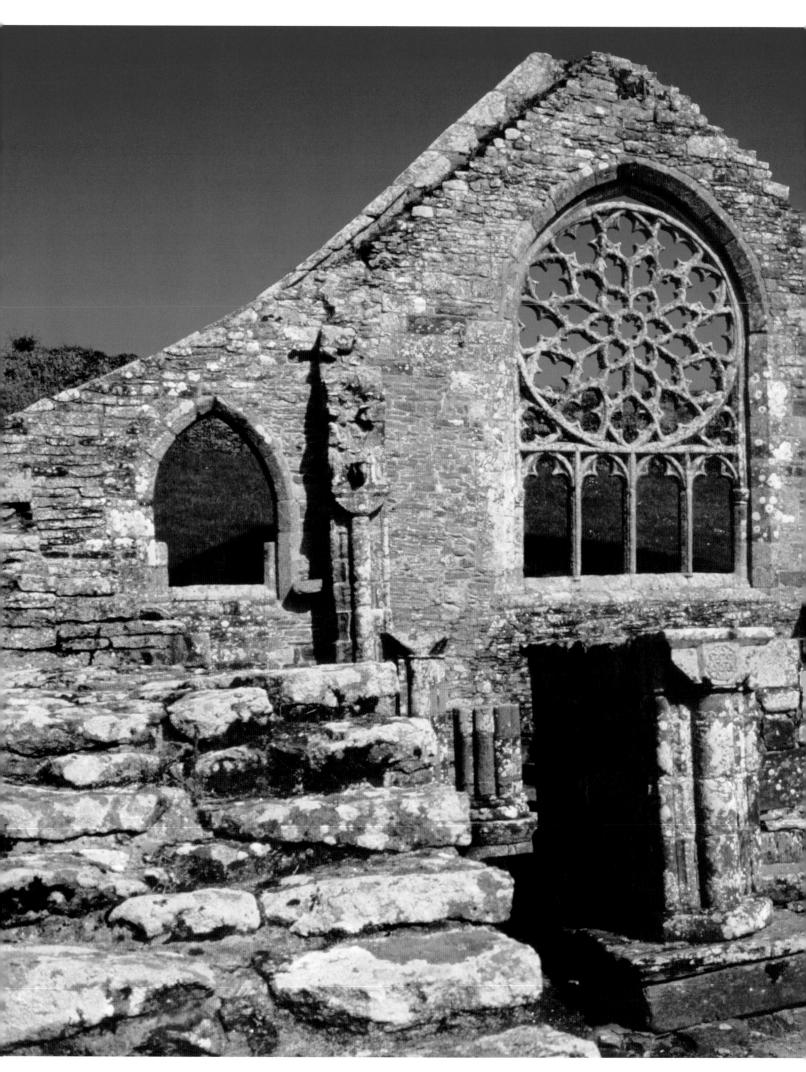

LEFT: Chapelle Langidou lies in ruins on a hilltop close to the pretty village of Piovan. It is believed to have been built in the thirteenth century.

BELOW: Looking like something straight from the pages of a storybook, Chateau d'Ussé is truly a breathtaking sight and a wonderful example of the many palaces that the Loire region has to offer. This particular chateau inspired Charles Perrault, the writer, to pen the classic fairytale "Sleeping Beauty."

PAYS DE LOIRE, POITOU-CHARENTES, AND CENTRE

Hugging the Western side of France are the three regions of Pays de la Loire, Centre (containing many of the Loire départements), and Poitou-Charentes. Despite their proximity, these regions could not be less alike in outlook, appearance or history.

The Pays de Loire and Centre regions of France are famed for beautiful, green valleys, winding rivers, and of course, the many impressive chateaux that are scattered across the area. The Loire Valley in Centre is often named "Chateau Country" and there is nowhere else in France that offers such a plethora of palaces. From as far back as the Middle Ages until the seventeenth century, the Loire province was home for the royal family. The stunning Chateau Chambord was the residence of many kings throughout the years, and where the king went, the noblemen followed, building their own impressive palaces. The Loire Valley soon became a playground for the rich and powerful. This era of excess continued after the Renaissance to such an extent that the mistress of King Henry II, Diane de Poitiers, used one of the most beautiful

chateaus in all the area, Chateau Chenonceau, purely as a pleasure palace. Many of the towns in the area were improved thanks to the attentions of the aristocracy. For example, the town of Gien was transformed by Anne de Beaujeu, daughter of Louis XI, who arranged for the building of the chateau, the bridge, the cloisters and the church. Without these the town would be a less picturesque place.

Back in the thirteenth century, Orléans, the capital of Centre, was the intellectual center of the country and its status was reflected in its appearance. Unfortunately, this once magnificent city, birthplace of Joan of Arc, was bombed relentlessly during World War II and little remains of its original splendor. There are however, many memorials and statues dedicated to the towns most famous daughter.

Poitou-Charentes is best described as "old school." The people's love of all things traditional is reflected in their buildings and their farming. Famed for both their oysters

and the brandy that bears its name, this is a charming and ageless haven. Despite its serenity, this area has played a pivotal role in French history. In an attempt to conquer the entire country, Muslim forces began invading France with frightening success. The tide finally turned here, near Poitiers, when the Gallic hero, Charles Martel, and his cavalry beat back the aggressors. Consequently ending any further incursions by the Muslim armies.

BELOW: Known throughout the world for the spirit that bears its name, Cognac's nearby hillsides are full of vineyards. According to local legend, something supernatural happens during the distillation process. After the cognac has been aged for two years in the oak barrels that add to its rich flavor, exactly two percent of the Cognac will have evaporated in each cask. The cellar masters refer to this as "la part des anges"— the angels' portion.

LEFT: The city of Angers, lying on the river Maine, was once the capital of Anjou and the seat of the Plantagenet's. The Chateau of Angers now houses one of the most famous fourteenth-century tapestries, The 350-feet long Apocalypse of St. John.

ABOVE: The town hall in Cognac is situated near the Musée de Cognac, where visitors can hear the town's history and of course learn the secret history of the town's most famous export.

PAGE 142–143: The Loire River winds its way slowly across the lush green countryside that was once the exclusive playground for kings and noblemen.

BELOW: In the gorgeous village of Aubterre sur Dronne is the underground church of Saint Jean. Situated on a cliff, overlooking the River Dronne, the church is carved out of the rock and the inside the main hallway the ceiling reaches a height of sixty feet.

beautiful

LEFT: Standing guard at the entrance of La Rochelle's busy port are three great alabaster towers. Constructed out of the local limestone in the fifteenth century, these great monoliths frame the harbor protectively, reflecting the sun's bright rays and giving the town its nickname of La Ville Blanche.

ABOVE: Situated on the largest of France's Atlantic islands, Chateau d'Oléron can be reached by a bridge from the mainland. The island is famed for its long sandy beaches and oyster beds.

PAGES 148–149: La Rochelle in Poitou-Charentes is still a vibrant seaport with an important history. French settlers used this port to set off to a new life in Montreal, Canada. It is known also as the "white city" or La Ville Blanche because of the bright limestone cliffs crowned with fourteenth-century towers, which often become luminous when the sun's rays reflect back off them.

RIGHT: Close to the town where Leonardo da Vinci has his final resting place, Chateau Amboise has had its share of bad luck. Charles VIII died here after banging his head on a doorway. Napoleon gave the chateau to one of his politicians, who promptly tore most of it down; World War II destroyed the rest. Now only the façade facing the river remains.

150

LEFT: St. Gatien Cathedral in Tours encapsulates a range of eras. The choir dates from the thirteenth century, the transept from the fourteenth, the nave and the west face from the fifteenth and sixteenth centuries. The town of Tours itself is sophisticated and appealing. Many cafés line the streets and well-kept and impressive public buildings raise the standard of their surroundings.

ABOVE: Along the Indré River is the idyllic moated chateau of Azay-le-Rideau. Originally built and owned by Philippa Lesbahy, wife of one of the royal treasurers, the chateau was eventually relinquished to King Francois I, when it was discovered that her husband had been using the royal coffers as freely as his own.

PAGE 154–155: The capital of Eure département in Centre, Bourges has an imposing cathedral and landscaped gardens. The gothic Cathédrale Saint-Étienne was built between 1195 and 1255 and was declared a World Heritage Site in 1995.

ABOVE: Moat and facade of Chateau de Saint-Loup in Poitiers. The town itself is full of beautiful buildings which are a testament to the financial aid that Eleanor of Aquitaine gave to this region in her lifetime.

RIGHT: In the tiny village of Trôo there are treasures to be found under the ground. This unassuming entrance is one of many that leads to vast subterranean dwellings, locally named *habitations troglodytiques*.

LEFT: During its long history, Chateau de Saumur has functioned as a prison, a stronghold and a country retreat. Originally built by Louis XI in 1246, unfortunately it recently began to collapse along its western side.

PAGE 160–161: The majestic Chateau Chambord has been called home by many kings throughout its great history. Originally started as a hunting lodge for Louis XIV, it developed into a huge palace with 365 fireplaces and windows, 70 stairways, and 450 rooms—not to mention a vast hunting estate with its own wild boar and Renaissance gardens.

ABOVE LEFT: The Chateau of Sully-sur-Loire is unusual as it has a fourteenth-century central fortress and a seventeenth-century wing added. The older part shows a slice of life from the Middle Ages where comfort and luxury were not yet considered indispensable. The newer section is more decorative and much warmer.

LEFT BELOW: One of a few remaining and well-kept chateaux in the Poitou-Charentes region, the seventeenth-century Roche-Courbon castle was built just outside Rochefort in the middle of barren marshland. Kept as a luxurious residence by Jean-Louis de Courbon, it fell into disrepair after Revolution. It was eventually restored to its former glory in the midtwentieth century.

ABOVE: Just outside Poitiers the gleaming edifice of Futurscope juts out into the sky. This futuristic theme park is a great example of modern architecture, so much more dramatic when surrounded by the otherwise pastoral scenes that fill this area.

PAGE 164: The sixteenth-century gardens of Chateau Villandry are supposed to represent the four faces of love on one side and music on the opposite. The kitchen gardens are planted according to the traditions of medieval abbeys and flower in a different color though each season.

PAGE 165: In the quiet town of Neuvy-Deaux-Clochers stands the house of sculptor, Jean Linard. His garden holds many fine examples of his work using unusual materials such as tiles and glass.

LEFT: A twenty-six-year labor of love, this charming house completely covered in mosaics was the work of Raymonde Isidore, a manual laborer living in Chartres who worked tirelessly to transform his family home into this stunning work of art.

ABOVE: The interior of Chateau de Blois, home of former Queen Catherine de Medici. This is the luxurious gilt-edged bedroom of the famous royal.

RIGHT: The Manoir du Cloux, former home of Leonardo da Vinci. He took the appointment of first painter and architect to King Francis I in 1516. He lived here for three years until 1519, when he died aged 67.

AQUITAINE

AQUITAINE

Covering the southwestern side of France, Aquitaine consists of the five départements of Dordogne, Gironde, Landes, Lot-et-Garonne, and the Pyrénées-Atlantiques. During the time of Roman occupation in the fourth century A.D., Gallia Aquitania covered an area almost one third the size of France and unlike its Northern counterparts, Aquitaine took to the cultures and customs of the Roman invaders. When the Romans left, the possession of the area passed from the Visigoths and then to the Franks in 507 A.D. Unfortunately, after the death of King Clotaire II or Clotaire the Good in 629, the Frankish hold on the region began to slip and they were soon ousted by Moorish invaders. After the hero, Charles Martel, banished the Muslim forces in the eighth century, control of the province passed back into French hands. Things remained this way until Eleanor of Aquitaine had her marriage to Louis VII annulled (on the grounds that they were related) and married the English king, Henry II, in 1152. Eleanor was responsible for much of the rejuvenation across France and under her guiding hand many towns and cities were built or improved. Aquitaine remained under English control for another three centuries until 1453 when France reclaimed it after the Hundred Years War.

Nowadays Aquitaine is peaceful refuge for many people, in fact this area is one of the most popular for foreign house buyers, especially the English. The landscape has everything, from rural farmland and undulating valleys, to white sandy beaches or soaring mountain ranges. The capital city of Bordeaux is famous the world over for its wines. In this area of the country are approximately around 500 square miles of vineyards containing 57 appellations with 9,000 chateaux (the wine-makers).

To the south of Aquitaine is the Pays Basque—Basque Country, a wild untamed land full of fiercely independent people who cling to their unique heritage and language.

Ancient Roman documents dating back to the fifth century mention a mysterious tribe called the Vascones, who lived in that same region of France. The Basques have occupied this area since the sixth century A.D. and ruled themselves fairly successfully throughout the Middle Ages until the French Revolution. Since then a small section of people have been striving to achieve a separate Basque state.

The language of the Basques, Euskara, is unique in that it has remained untouched by the influences of Latin and any of its modern offshoots. Many linguists have studied it but have been unable to trace its origins and can find no similar language on Earth.

PREVIOUS PAGES: The popular coastal town of Biarritz was an unassuming place until the middle of the nineteenth century when Empress Eugénie and Napoleon III visited and immediately made it a retreat for the elite by building a palace on the beach—now known as the Hotel du Palais. It remains a haven for the rich and famous to this day.

LEFT: Clouds roll over from the surrounding mountains, enveloping the pretty town of Castet, in the Basque region of the Pyrénées-Atlantiques .

ABOVE: Aquitaine, and especially the Dordogne, attracts thousands of foreign settlers every year. Delightful houses such as this are plentiful and quickly snapped up. In fact, there are now so many English settlers in the Dordogne, that the local French have started jokingly calling it "Dordogneshire."

BELOW: Aquitaine is famed for its many vineyards and in the Bordeaux area alone there are 444 square miles of vines. But the wine-making industry sweeps the length of Aquitaine and here, near Bergerac in the Dordogne, is Chateau Monbazillac. This sixteenth-century Renaissance castle is the home of the rich red wine that shares its name.

ABOVE: The romantic ruins of Commerque Castle stand on a high hilltop overlooking the valley beneath. Underneath the castle is a cave where prehistoric cavemen have carved animals on the walls.

RIGHT: The Pyrennees are home to the Pottok ponies. These formerly wild ponies are thought to have been in the area up to ten thousand years ago as they are represented in local cave drawings. Nowadays there are only a few thousand left, and all are owned rather than wild.

BELOW: This aerial view of the Lot-et-Garonne area of Aquitaine is a typical example of the local geography. Most of the region is farmland that ranges across undulating valleys. At any given time here, there could be fields covered in sunflowers, orchards full of plum trees (a local speciality—Agen prunes are thought to be the best), or grape vines as far as the eye can see.

174

LEFT: The Dordogne River winds it way through lush green valleys and past many ancient chateaux. During the Hundred Years War the river acted as a boundary line between French- and English-held France.

PAGE 178: Hanging decorations festoon the Cathédrale de St. Front in Périgueux. This imposing edifice was first built in the twelfth century and then almost completely destroyed and rebuilt in the nineteenth century. The new church now has five domes and seventeen towers, as well as the original bell tower. The finished result resembles a mosque or a Chinese temple.

PAGE 179: In the language of the area Bayonne means good river and the River Ardour still shapes the town of Bayonne to this day—separating the sleepy and more Basque area of Petit Bayonne from the older area known as Grande Bayonne. In this ancient part of the city stand the twin towers of Cathédrale Ste. Marie. Work began on the cathedral in the thirteenth century when this region was under English rule, but it was not completed until 1451 when the French had regained control. As a result, the cathedral is decorated with both English and French emblems.

RIGHT: Saint-Cirq-Lapopole on the edge of the River Lot perches on a clifftop, overlooking the flowing landscape beneath. The village was rescued from general decay and ruin when celebrated poet, André Breton, came to live here and waxed about its beauty in his works.

PAGE 182: The imposing Chateau Beynac stands high on a cliff overlooking the Dordogne River and staring across the gulf towards Chateau de Castelnaud. Although held by opposing armies during the Hundred Years War, the two castles have fared well and Chateau Beynac is one of the best and most beautifully restored examples of a twelfth-century keep.

PAGE 183: Saint-Cirq-Lapopole on the edge of the River Lot perches on a clifftop, overlooking the flowing landscape beneath. The village was rescued from general decay and ruin when celebrated poet, André Breton came to live here and waxed about its beauty in his works.

LEFT: The picture-perfect market town of Sarlat in the Dordogne valley was the capital of Black Périgord (called "black" because of the abundance of truffles in the area). This charming place has small criss-crossing streets that seem to encapsulate the idea of a perfect French town. It has often been used as a movie set for just this reason.

ABOVE: On the Basque coast of the Old Port in Biarritz sits La Villa Belza. The unique construction was first erected in 1880 and has been carefully maintained, in spite of the proximity of the pounding ocean waves and salty air.

PAGE 186–187: Here in the stunning yet rugged area of the Pyrénées-Atlantiques lies the region known as Pays Basque. This part of France has its own distinct language, with a quarter of residents speaking Basque or Euskara. They have a markedly different culture, but nevertheless, consider themselves as a part of France. The countryside is dotted with ruined towns and forts and many romantic villages nestle into the hillsides.

ABOVE: Makers of one of the most well-known dessert wines in the Bordeaux region, Chateau y'Quem is just one of the thousands of vintners in the province of Aquitaine.

RIGHT: Situated in the Gironde estuary is the Bassin d'Arcachon. Just along from this small coastal town is the Dune de Pilat—the longest sand dune in Europe.

BELOW: Chateau de Bonaguil in the Lot-et-Garonne was the last medieval castle to be built in France. Construction began in 1483 and took forty-three years to complete. It was built for Baron Berenger of Roquefeuil who wanted a protective stronghold, he certainly got it. The castle had thirteen towers and close to 1,300 feet of defensive walls.

LEFT: Built in 1489, the Chateau de Milandes is nestled in the heart of the Dordogne valley. It was extensively restored by a rich industrialist at the beginning of the twentieth century, who added many of the more romantic touches—such as the turrets and gables. A spectacle in its own right, the main draw to the chateau is its link with the famous singer, Josephine Baker. She rented Milandes in 1938 and was so enamored with it, nine years later she bought it for herself. The chateau now houses a museum dedicated to its most famous owner.

ABOVE: Belcastel in the Dordogne has been named one of France's most beautiful villages, and it is easy to see why. The once-ruined castle sitting high above the village fell into terrible disrepair until it was bought by the architect Fernand Pouillon. He single-handedly restored the site to its former glory and thus inspired the villagers to do the same with their own homes. Since his death in 1986, the village has continued his work and the village and chateau stand as a testament to his vision.

BURGUNDY

BURGUNDY

There was a time during Burgundy's illustrious history, that it appeared it would conquer all of France. In the fourteenth and fifteenth centuries, the duchy of Burgundy stretched all the way up through Holland and Luxembourg and it was one of the wealthiest and most powerful regions in Europe. There was little love lost between the two opposing countries, with machinations and power plays on both sides. In fact, Joan of Arc, the archetypal heroine of France, was sold to the English by Burgundy. Eventually the duchy of Burgundy fell under French rule in 1477 and the area, though much diminished in size, has lost none of its stature.

The capital of Burgundy, Dijon, is a sophisticated and cultural city full of medieval and renaissance buildings,

many of them are bedecked with colorful roof tiles—as is traditional in this part of France. Dijon has been the capital of Burgundy since the eleventh century, and many of its rulers have helped to improve the look of the city. During its zenith, in the fourteenth and fifteenth centuries, Dijon was home to many great kings, including Philip the Bold (Phillipe-le-Hardi), John the Fearless (Jean-sans-Peur), and Philip the Good (Phillipe-le-Bon). These forward-thinking kings invited some of the best artists, sculptors, and architects to enrich the capital, making Dijon one of the finest-looking cities in all France.

Burgundy was also a great epicenter for religion and two of the most important monastic orders were situated here. The Cistercian monks had an abbey at Citeaux and the

Benedictines had an abbey at Cluny. Although most of the abbey at Citeaux has been destroyed, it is still possible to visit the remains of the abbey at Cluny.

Of course the thing that Burgundy is best known for is its wine, and in the Côte d'Or (meaning Hills of Gold) region, the best way to explore this by following the Route des Grands Crus. This gently meandering road sways in and out of tiny medieval villages, past ancient chateaux and of course, through copious vineyards. Here, thirsty visitors are encouraged to sample the best wines and learn about the methods used in making them.

One supremely French national pastime is strongly linked to Burgundy—the consumption of escargots. The preferred species of snail is called the *Helix pomatia*—or to give it its more common name, the Burgundy Snail. Once abundant in this part of the world, their numbers have dwindled due to over-use of pesticides and over-harvesting. Nowadays most snails eaten in France are imported from Greece and Eastern Europe.

PREVIOUS PAGES: The Benedictine monastery situated on hilltop near the peaceful town of Vézelay contains the relics of Mary Magdalene; because of this it was a popular site for pilgrims during the eleventh and twelfth centuries. It was here that Saint Bernard sermonized on the Second Crusade, and Richard the Lionheart and King Philip Augustus met before embarking on the Third Crusade. Vézelay remains an untouched slice of history and is now a protected World Heritage Site.

BELOW LEFT: This medieval hospital in Dijon is ornamented with a fine display of the decorative roof tiles so popular throughout this area.

BELOW: Considered by many locals to be the true heart of the Côte d'Or, Beune enjoys a thriving Saturday market, where the most important produce is, naturally, wine.

PREVIOUS PAGES: One of the many vineyards available to view along the Route des Grands Crus. The Côte d'Or stretches nearly forty miles from the Côtes de Nuits in the north, which produces full-bodied red wines, all the way to the southern region of Côtes de Beaune, known for its reds and whites.

LEFT: Sitting on a hilltop overlooking the Armançon River is the town of Semur-en-Auxois. One of the last outposts of Gaulish rebellion until eventually defeated by the Romans, inside the thirteenth-century church of Notre Dame, the windows of a chapel commemorate American soldiers of World War I—Semur was the general headquarters of the U.S. 78th Division.

PAGE 202: Originally built in 1118, this carefully restored Cistercian abbey reveals the day-to-day lifestyle of the monks who once lived here. Possessing a simple church, bare dormitories, and a landscaped garden and arboretum—all sitting amid a serene valley—the Abbaye de Fontenay demonstrates the joys of a life devoted to quiet contemplation.

PAGE 203: The Abbey of St. Philibert in Tournus was reconstructed after a fire in the eleventh century. The abbey was not completed until 1120, over a hundred years later. Built from a rose-colored stone, the interior is beguiling in its simplicity and the recently restored crypts are adorned with frescos depicting the life of St. Philibert.

PREVIOUS PAGES: The quiet town of Autun used to be one of the most important places in Roman-occupied Gaul. It had within its defensive walls an ampitheater, four colossal gateways, and aqueducts. Unfortunately, on the Romans' departure, the city was ravaged by thieves and fell into disrepair. By the Middle Ages, some of the city's luck had changed and it slowly made a recovery. Now it boasts a fine cathedral called the Cathédrale St.-Lazare (pictured). Built in the twelfth century, it contains the holy relics of Saint Lazarus.

RIGHT: Sitting prettily on the Burgundy Canal is the small village of Vandesses-en-Auxois. The Canal is 150 miles long, has 209 locks, and was originally built to join the Atlantic ocean to the Mediterranean. Work on the canal began in 1727 and was finished by 1832.

PAGE 208: The Ducal Palace in Nevers is one of the finest examples of a feudal building in France. The outside windows are decorated with sculptures that tell the story of the house of Cleves, the family which built the majority of this building.

PAGE 209: The Chapel of Berze La Ville was built in the 1100s by Saint Hugh and is famed for its many well-preserved frescos which adorn the walls and ceilings. Burgundy contains a plethora of religious buildings thanks to the proximity of powerful and protective monastic orders, which deterred the Barbarian hordes that often defiled other, less sheltered, Christian churches.

ABOVE: The view across Dijon from the Philip-le-Bon tower in the Palais des Ducs. This fifteenth century construction is 150 feet high and the locals swear that from it on a sunny day they can see all the way to Mont Blanc.

RIGHT: The once great Benedictine Abbey in Cluny was the largest Christian church in the world until the completion of the Basilica of St. Peter in Italy. Nowadays there is very little remaining of the original buildings, just a few scattered ruins which give the impression of a once-magisterial structure.

PREVIOUS PAGES: Dating as far back as the twelfth century, Chateau de Rully has belonged to the same family since its construction. It is now a major wine maker in the Burgundy region.

RIGHT: Close to Beaune is the town and chateau of La Rochepot. The chateau was built in the eleventh century by Alexander of Burgundy, but virtually destroyed in the French Revolution. Fully restored in the nineteenth century by Sadi Carnot —once president of the republic—it has many impressive treasures, including a Chinese room, a bedroom full of oriental treasures gifted by the last empress of China to Carnot.

PAGE 216: The Basilica Sacré Coeur in Paray-le-Monial is famed throughout Christendom for the tale of Marguerite-Marie Alacoque (1647–90), a nun who claimed Jesus appeared to her and showed her his heart that loved all men. Since that time, the church plays host to many pilgrims from across the world and the remains of the now-sainted nun lie in a decorated tomb at the rear of the basilica.

PAGE 217: During the autumn, the vineyards across Burgundy turn from deep green to a rich golden hue. It is easy to see why this area is called the Côte d'Or or hills of gold.

ABOVE: The Basilica of La Madeleine in Vézelay has had an unfortunate history. Over the years it has been attacked by the Huguenots in 1569, desecrated during the revolution, and even hit by lightning a few times. It was finally saved by architect Viollet-le-Duc. His restoration of the church breathed new life into the town of Vézelay.

ABOVE RIGHT: Erected between 1220 and 1240, the Église Notre Dame in Dijon is an extravagantly decorated building. Not only are the three levels adorned with numerous gurning gargoyles and the roof a kaleidescope of color, but the top of the church has the Horloge Jacquemart, a fourteenth-century clock taken from Flanders by Philip the Bold as a token of war.

BELOW RIGHT: Outside the town of Autun is the Roman theater—the ruins of a once-immense amphitheater built to seat sixteen thousand spectators.

LIMOUSIN AND AUVERGNE

BELOW: From the summit of the colossal and awe-inspiring Puy Mary there is a breathtaking view over the Auvergne valleys. Formed from an extinct volcano, this area is rich in dormant volcanoes and even has a theme park devoted to the subject, Puy Mary measures in at nearly 6,000-feet high.

LIMOUSIN AND AUVERGNE

espite Limousin's majestic beauty, its untamed hills are often overlooked due to the more pastoral landscapes of the nearby Dordogne. While it does not possess as many tourist attractions, it is a charming area nevertheless. Limousin contains the three départements of Haute-Vienne, Creuse, and Corrèze. The capital of the region is Limoges, a name synonymous with fine ceramics and porcelain—the city contains several museums devoted to its most famous export. Limoges has been a forerunner in the making of fine porcelain since the late eighteenth century, when local potters attempted to use ancient Chinese techniques. Limoges porcelain differs from any other in three important ways: it is white, extremely hard, and translucent. It is manufactured using kaolin (a white clay), quartz, and feldspar

Limousin also lays claim to the best carpets and tapestries in France. For more than five centuries the small market town of Aubusson, forty-five miles southeast of Limoges, has been hailed for its intricate and colorful carpets and tapestries. As far back as the 1600s Aubusson's weaving has been coveted by royalty and aristocracy from all over Europe. Unfortunately, the vibrant colors and elaborate design of items that were purely decorative did not meet with the approval of the Revolutionaries and many of the finer pieces were destroyed, along with a great many workshops. Nowadays the industry is booming again, with no fewer than thirty workshops operating in and around Aubusson—with exciting new designers, for example Jean Lurçat and Sylvaine Dubuisson, breathing new life into an ancient art.

The Auvergne is a rich and imposing area with many extinct volcanoes. Carpeted in dense forests, the mineral-rich volcanic soil ensures a profusion of lush vegetation. Although a quieter part of the country now devoted to healthy outdoor pursuits such as hiking, cycling or hang-gliding, at one point the outcome of French history hung on a pivotal moment that took place in these very hills. In 52 B.C. the chief of the Arveni tribe, Vercingétorix, very nearly halted Julius Caesar's conquest of Gaul. In spite of Caesar's attempts to keep all the Gaulish tribes fighting one another and therefore unable to defend against a Roman invasion, Vercingétorix rallied all the tribes together and led

them to a glorious victory. The Roman forces were decimated in battle at Gregoria. Vercingétorix kept on beating back Caesar's troops for the following few years, using a mixture of guerrilla warfare and open battle. Eventually the Romans stemmed the flow of rebellion and Vercingétorix was captured, bound, and paraded through Rome in humiliation. He died in a Roman prison six years later.

One of the most impressive sights, and completely unique to this area, is the sprawling Parc Naturel des Volcans d'Auvergne. This 1,525-square mile national park has some of the most spectacular views from the summits of extinct volcanoes. The Monts Dômes, for example, are a succession of eighty cinder cones culminating in the towering Puy de Sancy, the park's highest point at 6,184 feet.

LEFT: The Grottes de Rouffignac are a series of tunnels made by an underground river. The tunnels contain many fascinating prehistoric drawings. This one is of a wooly rhinoceros, although mammoths are a speciality also.

ABOVE: The quiet riverside town of Aubusson is famed throughout France for its tapestries. The town boasts a cultural center devoted to the subject and named after the artist whose work rejuvenated the tapestry industry —Jean Lurçat.

PAGE 224–225: Perched on the summit of a lava tower some 275-feet-high stands the Chapelle St. Michel d'Aiguilhe. Situated in the heart of Le Puy-en-Vellay, this tenth-century church is only reached by hiking up 276 steep stairs.

PAGE 226: Le Puy-en-Vellay is surrounded by three enormous towers of lava. The highest is crowned with the Rocher Corneille, a fifty-foot-high statue of the Virgin Mary and child. Dating from 1860, this crimson icon was made from melted-down cannon used in the Crimean War.

PAGE 227: Now a protected historic monument, Chateau Montbrun has had a chequered past. Originally built in the twelfth century by the Brun family, it has been held by the English during the Hundred Years War, attacked by Protestants during the Wars of Religion, ravaged by fire, and pillaged during the French Revolution. Nowadays it leads a more serene life, as a hotel.

RIGHT: This fifteenth-century fortress sits on a rocky outcrop of Lake Bort, in the heart of the volcano region of Limousin. Chateau de Val overshadows all else around it.

PAGE 230: During World War II, the sleepy town of Oradour-sur-Glane was like any other until the afternoon of June 10, 1944, when SS troops gathered the entire population in the town square. The men were locked in barns which were then set alight; the women and children locked in the church with a ticking bomb. Anyone trying to escape was shot. Out of 642 inhabitants, only six survived. The village has been kept untouched to this day—a stark visual reminder of the atrocities of war.

PAGE 231: Positioned high on a hilltop above the River Vezère is the quiet town of Uzerche. The town is well-known for its fifteenth-century Maisons à Tourelles, houses that look like diminutive castles mainly because of their turrets and towers.

PREVIOUS PAGES: Voted as one of the most beautiful in all of France, the medieval village of Curemont in Limousin dates from the eleventh century and can lay claim to no fewer than three castles.

ABOVE: The Fortresse de Polignac in the Auvergne still belongs to the once-influential Polignac family. From the eleventh to the fourteenth century this clan ruled over Velay from their mountainous keep. Now greatly restored, visitors can still visit the hundred-foot-high chateau balanced on an even taller volcanic outcrop.

RIGHT: One of the best and easiest ways to enjoy the splendors in and around Le Puy-en-Vellay is by floating above the town in a hot-air balloon.

PAGES 236–237: The picturesque village of Saint-Arcons-d'Allier, surrounded by the lush green countryside that Auvergne is so famed for. The rich volcanic soil ensures verdant forests and plentiful crops.

ABOVE: The chapel of St. Michel d'Aiquilhe stands on an ancient volcano vent high above the terra cotta rooftops of Le Puy.

ABOVE RIGHT: Overlooking the Sioule River, the remains of the thirteenth-century Chateau de Rocher are an impressive sight even now. Built originally by the lords of Bourbon, the castle is now a protected heritage site.

RIGHT: Presented as a gift by Louis XV to his favored concubine, Madame Pompadour, Chateau Arnac-Pompadour never housed its new mistress. Instead it now accommodates one of the most famous stud farms in the world, where Anglo-Arabian horses were first bred. Horse races are held here every summer.

LEFT: This fifteenth-century mountain keep was built by Louis d'Anjony who was one of Joan of Arc's *compagnons*—meaning master builders. It was originally commissioned by King Charles VII to protect the surrounding countryside.

ABOVE: The imposing Chateau de Rochebaron dominates a valley over the gorges of the Loire. Built by the lords of Rochebaron during the eleventh century, the castle fell into disrepair under Louis XIV but efforts have been made in the local community since 1987 to restore it to its former glory.

PAGES 242–243: An aerial view over the terra-cotta rooftops of Le Puy to the mountains in the distance.

241

PARIS AND ITS OUTSKIRTS

Known worldwide as the city of love, art, and café culture, the home of all things chic, Paris is a city unlike any other. The history of Paris exudes from every street with thousands of monuments and ancient buildings whispering its story through the ages.

The first settlers in what is now France's capital city were a small tribe of Celts known as the Parisii. They set up home on what is now called the Ile de la Cité, the oldest part of modern Paris.

When the Romans arrived in 52 B.C. they rechristened the town Lutetia, but the name did not stick, and after the Romans' departure in the fifth century, it reverted back to Paris. The Franks quickly took over control of the city. King Clovis I united the country and made Paris his new capital. Many famous monuments were erected in the following years. The twelfth century saw the construction of Notre Dame cathedral, and the Louvre was originally built in the thirteenth century as a fortress. The famed Sorbonne began taking students in 1253.

During the Hundred Years War, King Henry VI of England was crowned King of France inside Notre Dame in 1430, but twenty-three years later the English were ousted from France and a new French king crowned.

The royal line was to come to an end three centuries later, seventy-five years after the reign of one of France's most famous monarchs, Louis XIV, the Sun King. The excesses of King Louis XVI (1754–1793) and his queen, Marie Antoinette, led to an uprising of angry Parisians on the night of July 14, 1789, and the famed storming of the Bastille. The revolution, though led by a fair and just council at first, quickly degenerated into the Reign of Terror, a four-year period where no one was safe from "Madame Guillotine." Even Robespierre, one of the early revolutionary leaders, was to meet his maker under her steely gaze. Eventually the atmosphere of the country stabilized under the rule of Napoleon Bonaparte and in 1804 he had himself crowned emperor in Notre Dame Cathedral. After this he captured half of Europe but his unceasing ambition was to be his downfall. After ignominious defeats in Russia (1812), then again at Waterloo (1815), he was exiled to the remote island of Elba where he died in 1821.

It was under Napoleon III—the nephew of Bonaparte who seized power in 1848—that major changes next took place in the city. Napoleon III was a man of vision with plans for France's capital. To make Paris a city to be proud of, he hired Baron Haussmann. Not an architect by trade but an expert organizer, Haussmann consulted with engineers and architects, and set about his task with vigor. He demolished 27,000 houses and built 100,000 more; he made the wide boulevards—so identifiably Parisian today; established a working sewer system and water works; built

enough schools, churches, and prisons for a major growing capital; and added the beautiful Bois de Boulogne.

However, not all of Napoleon's plans were positive. His ill-advised war with the Prussians led to his defeat and capture. Following this France declared itself a republic once more.

Paris of the late nineteenth century was a glitzy center for hedonism. Zidler opened the notorious Moulin Rouge, Paris welcomed the world's first strip club nearby, and champagne flowed like water.

War soon ended this carefree time and both world wars took an extreme toll on Paris, particularly during the occupation of World War II. Following the fall of France in 1940, the young general Charles de Gaulle headed the Free French government in exile in London, while German soldiers basked in the champagne lifestyle of Paris.

As the end of the war approached and Paris' liberation seemed imminent, Hitler ordered the city destroyed on August 23, 1944. His right-hand-man in Paris, Von Choltitz, did not carry out the order and his hesitation saved the city as we know it today and earned him a commendation from the French government. By August 25, Charles de Gaulle was paraded down the streets of the city in victorious applause. Paris was finally free.

Since then Paris has grown in population and has embraced its reputation as a city of art and culture. Paris now boasts both the rich evocative buildings of the old alongside some of the most adventurous and unique architectural ventures of the present.

PREVIOUS PAGES: A world-famous Parisian nightclub, the Moulin Rouge welcomed its first bon-viveurs in 1889. It was immortalized by the painter Toulouse-Lautrec, making the can-can the most celebrated of all French dances.

LEFT: Paris in the 1700s was becoming clogged with the remains of its dead, so a macabre yet effective plan was formed to deal with the problem. Cemeteries across Paris were dug up and the remains transferred to the tunnels of three ancient quarries. The catacombs beneath Montparnasse contain millions of skulls and bones, and markers show where each carefully piled stack originally came from.

ABOVE: The Latin Quarter is a vibrant and friendly part of Paris, famed for its diverse choice of restaurants and bars. When night falls, the cobbled streets come to life with restaurant owners touting for business on the steps of their establishments, trying to tempt in any passing customer.

ABOVE: The exterior walls of Notre Dame Cathedral are covered in demonic gargoyles. From the summit of the north tower, some 387 spiraling steps upward, the most frightening examples look out over the Paris skyline.

RIGHT: The Colonne de Juillet stands in the center of the Place de la Bastille. The figure of Liberty stands on top of the bronze column. It was erected in 1833 as a memorial to all those who died during the revolution of 1830.

PAGE 250: Built by King Louis XIV in 1679, Hôtel des Invalides was home to over 4,000 disabled war veterans. However, its place in history was cemented on July 14, 1789, when the building was stormed by an angry mob, who captured 28,000 rifles and went on to attack the Bastille Prison, thus beginning the French Revolution. The sparkling Église du Dôme holds the remains of Napoleon.

PAGE 251: A poignant example of one of the many beautiful gravestones inside the Montparnasse cemetery. A haunting bronze angel crawls over the top of a child's grave.

LEFT: The Palais Garnier in the Opéra arrondissment of Paris was built during the nineteenth century and is one of the most impressive opera houses in Paris. The lush interior is gilded in gold and rich red velvet, and it regularly shows ballets, operas, and classical music concerts.

PAGE 254: Sculpture in front of the supremely Gothic Église St.-Eustache in Les Halles. The church is dedicated to a Roman martyr and the patron saint of hunters. Erected between 1532 and 1640, it stands next to the gardens at Forum des Halles.

PAGE 255: The majestic Notre Dame Cathedral on the Ile de la Cité stands on the site of an ancient Gallo-Roman temple. Constructed between 1168 and the 1300s, it is famed for its perfect symmetry and spectacular art-glass windows. Although, looking closely, it is clear that there are small asymmetrical touches—as was the Gothic style—in an effort to stop the building becoming too repetitive.

PREVIOUS PAGE: The Trocadero Fountains opposite the Eiffel Tower take their name from a Spanish stronghold close to Cadiz that was seized by the French in 1823. When the fountains are illuminated at sunset and they transform into one of the most romantic places in Paris.

ABOVE: The oldest church in Paris, the Église St.-Germain des Prés, was erected in the eleventh century on the site of a sixth-century abbey. Until the completion of Notre Dame, St.-Germain des Prés was the foremost church in France.

RIGHT: La Geode Cinema in the Parc de la Villette is covered in 6,500 stainless steel tiles which reflect the area around it to remarkable effect. Inside is a 360-degree cinema which shows educational movies on space, travel and the natural world.

PAGE 260–261: The sprawling grounds of Père-Lachaise Cemetery are now "home" to many famous poets, writers, and singers. The cemetery opened its doors in 1824 and since then it has welcomed Baudelaire, Samuel Beckett, Jean Seberg, Jean-Paul Satre, Simone de Beauvoir, and perhaps the most visited of all, Jim Morrison, into its boundaries.

ABOVE: Construction of the Basilisque du Sacré Coeur in Montmartre began in 1873 as an act of contrition for the horrors of the ill-advised Franco-Prussian war. The war began in 1870, the brainchild of the over-ambitious Napoleon III. It was to lead to his capture and the loss of the emperor's throne.

RIGHT: The most recognizable creation in all of Paris is the Eiffel Tower. Named after its architect, Gustave Eiffel, it is over a thousand feet high and made from 10,000 tons of iron. Hated by Parisians when it first arrived, it was almost torn down in 1909. Fortunately it was saved due the burgeoning technology of radio, as it was an ideal place for a transmitter. These days 5.8 million visitors climb to the summit each year to enjoy the giddy view.

BELOW: Linking the Hotel des Invalides to the Champs Elysées, the Alexandre III bridge is named after the Russian Tsar and celebrates the Russo-French alliance of the late nineteenth century.

PAGE 264–265: The pink granite obelisk standing in the Place de la Concorde is estimated to be 3,300 years old. It originally stood in the Temple of Ramses in Thebes but was gifted to France in 1831 by Mohammad Ali—not the boxer but the pasha of Eygpt. During the French Revolution a guillotine stood on this spot and over 1,300 people lost their heads here, including Marie-Antoinette and Louis XVI.

ABOVE: The breathtaking golden interior of the Palais Garnier. The opera house is often referred to as the most beautiful in all Paris.

LEFT: Standing in the center of the world's biggest roundabout is the Arc de Triomphe. Commissioned by Napoleon to celebrate his numerous victories, work began in 1806. The arc remained incomplete after Napoleon's fall. It was finally finished in 1836.

PAGE 268–269: A popular summertime stop for Parisians and visitors, the Jardin du Luxembourg is filled with chestnut groves and sculpted gardens. The palace was built as a home for Marie de Médici, the mistress of King Henri IV, but since 1958 it has been used by the French senate.

PAGES 270–271: The Palais du Louvre was originally constructed as a
fortress in the thirteenth century then rebuilt in the sixteenth century and
turned into a royal residence. It did not become a museum until 1793,
when the revolutionary committee took possession.

ABOVE: La Grande Arche in the La Défense district just outside Paris was completed in 1989 and is the centerpiece of a truly space-age setting. The arch is 360-feet long and built of white marble. It contains government offices and various businesses.

273

ABOVE: The Basilica of Saint Denis was the final resting place for much of France's royalty, and the ornate tombs held within are some of the finest examples in the world. The basilica is named after the patron saint of France, who introduced Christianity to the country. It is said that after he was beheaded by the Romans, he picked up his head, put it under his arm and walked up the hill chanting psalms to the very spot where the church now stands. A statue of the saint holding his freshly detached head is visible on the west portal of Notre Dame.

ABOVE RIGHT: Louis XIV dreamed up the palace at Versailles to illustrate the splendor that was the French monarchy. Thirty thousand men worked tirelessly on the chateau, the cost of which almost bankrupted the country.

RIGHT: The chateau at Fontainebleau lacks much of the overwhelming splendor of Versailles; instead, it is a more relaxed and sophisticated residence surrounded by acres of forest. There has been a chateau at this location since the twelfth century but the Renaissance chateau that stands now was built by François I in the fourteenth century and added to by subsequent rulers.

274

LEFT: The beautiful Chateau of Vaux-Le-Vicomte on the outskirts of Paris was built between 1656 and 1661 for the Minister of Finance, Nicolas Fouquet. Unfortunately this palace was to prove the death of him. So jealous of its perfection, the king, Louis XIV, had Fouquet thrown in jail, where he died almost twenty years later.

RIGHT: Les Deux Magots Café in the Saint Germain district is famous among literature fans. Jean Paul Sartre was a regular customer, as was Ernest Hemingway. The Café de Flore, next door, was often frequented by Simone de Beauvoir. It was a favorite haunt for many intellectuals and is often considered the birthplace of existentialism.

MIDI-PYRÉNÉES AND LANGUEDOC-ROUSSILLON

BELOW: The walled medieval town of Carcassonne was built in the thirteenth century and was one of the last Cathar fortresses. The Cathars were a fundamentalist Christian sect who preached fervently in the local dialect—not in Latin—and the Pope declared them heretics. They were hunted down and burned at the stake; this was one of their last strongholds. Now the only thing besieging this fairytale town are tourists: on average three and a half million every year.

MIDI-PYRÉNÉES AND LANGUEDOC-ROUSSILLON

Languedoc-Roussillon did not exist until the 1980s. It was formed when the regions of Bas-Languedoc, Haut-Languedoc, and Roussillon were merged. Bas-Languedoc is famed for its well-preserved Roman ruins, golden beaches, and bull-fighting, and is the biggest wine producer in France. Under Frankish rule until the twelfth century, Occitania (as it was then known) enjoyed a golden age. The locally spoken language, Occitan, was considered the most refined in southern France. All this was to change when Languedoc was formally incorporated into France. The king ruled the official language to be *langue d'oil*, the form of French spoken in the north and the antecedent of modern French.

The major towns are Nîmes and Montpellier. Nîmes is steeped in Roman history, and within its center are some of the best-preserved Roman buildings in all of France. The amphitheater, for example, dates back to 100 A.D. but is still mostly intact. Nîmes also has a wonderful temple, known as Maison Carrée dating from around 5 A.D., and the well-maintained Roman fountain garden.

The region of Haut-Languedoc is in sharp contrast to its southern sister. Covered in wild mountainous ground and sparsely populated, this is an area for outdoor activities. The stark limestone flats of the Grands Causse are popular for hiking, and the plummeting gorges of the Tarn river offer an ideal place for canoeing. Many national parks and nature reserves flourish in this area, including a Bison reserve, a wolf reserve (now home to over 100 wolves), and the Parc National des Cévennes that has successfully reintroduced red deer, beavers, and vultures into the area.

Roussillon, so close to Spain, has imported much of its neighbor's culture and traditions. Often called "French Catalonia," the country was ruled by Spain until 1640 when Catalonians both here and in Spain rebeled against their rulers. The main town of Perpignan underwent a siege lasting two years and only survived thanks to the support of the French. The fighting stopped in 1659 when Spanish and French rulers signed the Treaty of the Pyrenees, which definitively set out the borders of each country. Roussillon was annexed into France, which came as an unwelcome shock to many of the inhabitants.

The Midi-Pyrénées incorporates the départements of Ariège, Aveyron, Gers, Haute-Garonne, Hautes-Pyrénées, Lot, Tarn, and Tarn et Garonne. This region was also created in the 1980s, mainly to give its foremost city, Toulouse, an area in which to be a capital. Most of what is now the Midi-Pyrénées was ruled over by the Counts of Toulouse during the Middle Ages. The whole area became part of France after the counts were defeated by the French king in the thirteenth century and the entire county of Toulouse was taken apart.

LEFT: A familiar sight throughout the south of France, fields of sunflowers decorate the landscape. Sunflowers, in particular their multipurpose seeds, are one of the main crops of this area.

ABOVE: The town of Albi on the Tarn River is peaceful now, but during the King's and Pope's crusade against the Cathars, it witnessed horrors—including mass burnings at the stake of any heretics.

PAGE 282–283: Another view of the ancient walls of Carcassonne.

ABOVE: The vertiginous town of Rocamadour has been a site of pilgrimage for many travelers since the unspoiled body of Saint Amadour was found in its tomb in 1166. Even today, many people climb the steep pathways to the Chapelle Notre Dame to witness the allegedly miraculous power of the Black Madonna inside.

RIGHT: Les Arènes in Nîmes is a beautifully preserved Roman amphitheater, and unlike many other of its kind, it still retains the upper levels. A series of passages mean that the richer spectators, closer to the action in the lower seats, would never have to come into contact with the riff-raff seated in the upper levels (or cheap seats). Built in 100 A.D., it houses 24,000 people.

LEFT: The famous "Grotte Miraculeuse" (Miraculous Cave) in Lourdes is surrounded by many places of worship. The Basilica of the Rosary was built in 1883–1889 and replaced the original chapel on the site of the Madonna's appearances.

ABOVE: The octagonal bell tower of the St. Sernin Basilica in Toulouse. The church was built between 1080 and 1120 A.D. on the site of a fourth-century basilica which housed the body of Saint Sernin. He was the first bishop of Toulouse and was martyred when a pagan priest tied him to a bull and he was dragged around the city.

BELOW: A source of inspiration to many, the old waterfront town of Collioure is the smallest on the Côte Vermeille. Painters such as Matisse, Braque, and Picasso have captured its charm. Thanks to such illustrious visitors, the town now enjoys a reputation as a center for the arts and has thirty galleries.

LEFT: The remote village of Hauterive in the Tarn gorges is almost inaccessible to traffic due to the plummeting cliffs around it.

ABOVE: The famous Benedictine Abbey in Lagrasse, founded in 799 A.D. by Charlemagne, was once one of the most important in France. It sired 6 other abbeys, another 25 priories, and no fewer than 67 churches. Its position on the border of France and Aragon meant it played an important role in the politics of the time.

PAGE 292–293: The hillside village of Autoire in the Lot region is eight centuries old; unlike many others, it suffered little during the Hundred Years War. This was thanks to the powerful defenses of its surrounding castle, Saint Laurent.

PAGE 294: The mountaintop Abbey of St. Martin du Canigou still holds a working religious community to this day. The eastern half of the abbey was built in 1009 and the western half in 1026. Unfortunately, due to an earthquake in 1428 and the slow abandonment of the monks, it fell into ruin by the eighteenth century. Restoration, both architecturally and spiritually, began in 1952 and ended in 1983.

PAGE 295: Olargues, one of the most spectacular rural villages in France, sits serenely on the edge of the Jaur River. It has a bell tower dating from the tenth century and is situated inside the Natural Reserve of Haut-Languedoc.

RIGHT: The village of Dourbie on the River Tarn marks the beginning of the impressive Tarn gorges. This area is well-known for its fishing and rare birds, not to mention the often-traveled walk from here, through the gorges, all the way to Nant.

PAGE 298: The entrance to the Gouffre de Padirac is a plummeting shaft 250 feet deep. It leads to the Causses de Gramat, vast underground caves that were discovered in the thirteenth century and have some amazing stalactites and stalacmites formed over thousands of years. The word "gouffre" means deep hole or bottomless pit in French.

PAGE 299: The famed carved elm tree in Le Caylar. The artist Michel Chevray spent two thousand hours sculpting the once-dead elm situated in the town square, giving it a new lease of life and turning it into a splendid work of art.

PAGE 300–301: Construction of the Saint Just cathedral in Narbonne began in 1272 and is yet to be finished. The original plans for the church involved the demolition of the nearby town hall but the council would not allow it.

ABOVE: A field of lavender sweeps downward from the pretty town of Montfort in the Gers region. This sleepy rural town now hosts open air festivals in the grounds of its local castle, Esclingac.

RIGHT: The Abbey of St. Foy in Conques was built by the monks who lived here in the twelfth century. A no-frills, functional masterpiece of construction, it was an important stop for pilgrims on the way to Santiago de Compostela. One of its few decorative touches is a deep archway over the western portal portraying the Last Judgement. No fewer than 124 finely preserved figurines appear in the scene dating back to the twelfth century.

BELOW: Les Cevennes National Park in Lozère is a group of steep gorges covered in dense chestnut and mulberry forests. The mulberry was originally planted to provide food for the silkworms so essential for the thriving silk trade that sustained this area in the eighteenth century.

ABOVE: The underground labyrinth called Les Grandes Canalettes under the foothills of the Pyrenees was discovered in 1982 by Edmund Demoniac. The many enormous chambers and pathways forged by underground rivers today culminate in a fantastic light show in the massive auditorium, where visitors can see the many colorful mineral deposits illuminated to the majestic sounds of Bach, Strauss, and Pavarotti.

RIGHT: Hidden inside a rock face, this cunningly disguised hill fort dates back to the Hundred Years War and was used by the English as a lookout point. It is known locally as the Chateau des Anglais (of the English).

306

PROVENCE, ALPES, AND
THE CÔTE D'AZUR

BELOW: Along the coastal roads from Nice to Menton are some of the most wonderful views of the Côte d'Azur. Known locally as the "corniches," these roads run through towering hills and mountainous villages all the way to Monaco. The village of Roquebrune perches high on the summit of a hill overlooking the coast. The streets all lead to the local tenth-century castle and the famous French architect, Le Corbusier is buried in the local cemetery.

PROVENCE, ALPES, AND THE CÔTE D'AZUR

During their turbulent histories these three southern regions of France have been invaded and occupied many times. Were it not for the scattered remains of ruins indicating the once mighty presence of Greek, Roman, and even Celtic cultures, it would be hard to imagine this land as anything but a serenely peaceful paradise.

Provence was progressively settled by the Romans from the second century B.C., eventually becoming a province of the Roman Empire. Its azure skies, turquoise waters, and fields of lavender and sunflowers have been captured on canvas by the likes of Van Gogh, Cézanne, and Gaugin. In fact it is said that the sunlight in these areas of southern France is clearer and brighter than anywhere else. The bustling and vibrant capital of Marseilles is France's oldest city after Paris and is a melting pot of nearby cultures including French, Spanish, African, and Italian. The old port of Marseilles, originally named Massilia, was founded by Greek sailors in 600 B.C. and maintained strong Greek influence up to the tenth century. It eventually became part of France in the 1480s but still steadfastly retained its sense of individuality. This rebelliousness manifested itself during

the French Revolution in 1792 when 500 volunteers from Marseilles advanced northward to help defend Paris and sang the stirring march "La Marseillaise"—now adopted as the French national anthem.

The Côte d'Azur has been a place of admiration and inspiration for centuries. Visitors from Queen Victoria to today's glittering Hollywood stars have all enjoyed its golden beaches and swum in its crystal-clear waters. Painters such as Matisse, Renoir, and Picasso have attempted to capture its beauty on canvas. In fact, two of the twentieth century's most influential painters chose to spend their last years in Cannes; Pierre Bonnard (1867–1949) and Pablo Picasso (1881–1973). The capital, Nice, was established in 350 B.C. by the same Greek sailors who founded Marseilles. Initially named Nikaia (after Nike, the Greek goddess of victory) it was taken by the Romans in the first century. Many Roman ruins are still found in the area, including an amphitheater built to seat 10,000 people. Although occupied many times by the French during the nineteenth and eighteenth centuries, Nice did not officially become part of France until 1860.

BELOW: The gorgeous village of Les-Baux-de-Provence sits on a rocky plateau in the heart of the Alpilles. Listed as one of France's most beautiful villages, it has a rich history and although being a magnet for tourists, still looks like a medieval village frozen in time. The village fortress dates back to the eleventh century and from its turrets there is a fantastic view all the way to Marseilles.

BELOW: Situated on the Moyen Corniche is Eze, a small walled village just within walking distance of the Italian border. There is only one way into the town which is a haven for artists and quaint one-off stores. There is a steep pathway from Eze to its sister town of Eze-sur-Mer on the coast below.

PAGE 314: The serene village of Entrecasteaux clings to the Bresque River in the département of Var. The village is dominated by a seventeenth-century chateau which has some splendid landscaped gardens designed by André Le Nôtre, who also devised the gardens for the palace at Versailles.

PAGE 315: The Cathedral of St. Sauveur in Aix-en-Provence was built between 1285 and 1350. A collection of many different architectural styles, it reflects the tastes of many centuries. The chapels were added in the fourteenth and fifteenth centuries and the golden Baroque organ was put in during the eighteenth century.

RIGHT: The old port of Marseilles has been welcoming ships into its harbor for more than twenty-six centuries. Standing over the entrance to the Vieux Port are two forts, Bas Fort St.-Nicholas and Fort St.-Jean. In the center is the imposing Chateau d'If, the dungeon made infamous by Alexander Dumas' most popular work—*The Count of Monte Cristo*. Here we can see the area around the port whose maze of markets, shops, and cafes which echo the relaxed atmosphere of this ancient city.

LEFT: Fields of lavender stretching to the horizon are a familiar sight throughout the Côte d'Azur. The temperate climate is perfect for growing flowers all year round and the nearby town of Grasse has been the capital of the perfume industry since the sixteenth century.

ABOVE: Notre-Dame de la Garde in Marseilles was one of the most ambitious projects of the nineteenth century. The first stone was laid on September 26, 1852. It was not completed until 1893 after the death of one architect and the mysterious disappearance of another. It was the architect Henri Revoli who finally oversaw completion.

The tiny hilltop village of Gordes was a stronghold for the resistance during World War II. As a result, the entire village was destroyed and many of the inhabitants massacred by the German forces. Since then the village has received a Croix de Guerre for its bravery and has now been completely restored.

PAGE 322–323: When the papal seat was moved from Rome to Avignon in 1309 because of political unrest, the Palais des Papes was built to be the new Vatican. This huge fourteenth-century Gothic palace is the largest of its kind and is a testament to the wealth garnered by the resident popes during their time here. Even though Rome was later reestablished as the true home of Catholicism, Avignon remained under Papal rule until 1791.

ABOVE: Within walking distance of the Italian border, the quiet coastal town of Menton is reported to have the warmest weather in the area. The hills that enclose the town and trap the warm currents coming from the Mediterranean make a perfect microclimate for growing citrus fruits.

RIGHT: The Lac de Saint Croix in the Verdun département stretches over six miles in length and two miles across, it is famed for its beauty and a popular place for kayaking and sailing.

LEFT: A quiet village nestles into the mountainside in the Haute-Alpes region. Peace has not always reigned in these parts though; during World War II, German and Italian forces occupied this area and the mountains were used to hide many resistance fighters.

PAGE 328: Every year local villagers make a pilgrimage to a tiny chapel situated on the shores of the turquoise waters of Lac de Sainte Ann. They hold a mass to beg for a plentiful harvest and sufficient rain.

PAGE 329: The village of Castellane is tucked into the base of a gorge in the Grand Canyon du Verdon. The chapel Notre-Dame-du-Rock is perched high above the town on the site of a Roman fortress.

327

BELOW: Believed to be descended from prehistoric stock, the Camargue horses can only be found in this area of France. Traditionally the mount of local farm workers, they do not own the wild horses, instead they are known as "guardians" to the beasts. Each year the horses are rounded up, inspected, counted, and then returned to the wild. There are currently thirty herds of Camargue horses wandering the countryside.

CORSICA

CORSICA

The island of Corsica is a place of surprising variation. Encircled by almost 600 miles of spectacular coastline, including some 200 spotless sandy white beaches, it also has snow-capped mountains, sheer rock cliffs, shimmering tarns, miles of chestnut forests, orange groves, and olive plantations. It even possesses a small desert in the north of the island. Most of the countryside is carpeted with dense shrubs and sweet-smelling flowers known locally as "maquis." The locals are an attractive mix of French hospitality and Italian hot-blooded passion.

Corsica has not always been part of France. From the eleventh to the thirteenth century the Italian state of Pisa presided over the island. In 1284, the sworn enemy of Pisa —Genoa—captured Corsica and overthrew the Pisans. Due to its proximity to Africa and susceptibility to seaborne assaults, the Genoese built many coastal watchtowers and citadels for protection, many of which survive to this day.

After so many years under foreign rule, the Corsicans revolted in 1755 under the leadership of Pasquale Paoli. They were successful in ousting the Genoans and promptly

established the most democratic system in Europe at that time. That most Italian of traditions—the blood vendetta—was made illegal; schools and universities were opened; and the national emblem of the "Moor's Head" was assumed. Legend has it that the scarf tied across the Moor's head had originally been fastened over his eyes like a blindfold but the newly free Corsicans changed it to a head scarf to symbolize the new-found liberation of its people.

This liberation, unfortunately, was not permanent. Genoa handed its rights to the island over to King Louis XV of France in 1768 and the following year the Corsicans were crushed under the heels of the mighty French army. Corsica officially became part of France in 1769.

Corsica is also famed for being the birthplace of Napoleon Bonaparte. Born in the town of Ajaccio in 1769 to Corsican nobility, his parents sent him to be educated in

France with the hope he would be given a French title. Little did they realize he would achieve the title of emperor.

In 1975 the island was split into two départements, Corse-de-Sud (the southern half of the island) and Haute-Corse (the northern half). Corsica still fights for independence even today and in 2001 was granted permission by the French government to teach the Corsican language in school. Although the island would like more autonomy from France and often protests against French rule, this outcome seems unlikely in the near future. For the meantime, the whole of France is enriched by the inclusion of their cultures and the landscape of such an island paradise.

PAGE 332–333: Basking in the sunlight on a gently sweeping bay, Calvi epitomizes any Mediterranean seaside resort. In the distance is the towering summit of Monte Cinto. It was here in 1794 that, while fighting alongside the Corsicans against the Genoese, Horatio Nelson (then merely a captain) was injured and lost the sight in his right eye.

LEFT: The Chateau Fort rock formation in the Scandola Nature Reserve is just one of the many interesting structures here. There are also numerous caves and coves to explore—there is even a rock that looks just like a dog's head!

PAGE 336–337: The quaint coastal town of Ile Rousse or Isula Rossa on the northern coast of Corsica is named after the red granite island of Ile de la Pietra which stands just off the shoreline. Now connected to the mainland, this thriving port was established by Pasquale Paoli in 1758 to contend with Calvi, which still supported the Genoese.

LEFT: Corsica is covered in steep mountains that remain blanketed in snow all year round, despite its Mediterranean location.

ABOVE: Forged by glaciers, the vertiginous Gorges de la Restonica near Corte are a popular location for hikers. Running through a superb forest of Larico pine, the River Restonica winds through the rocky outcrops creating many mountain lakes and bubbling streams.

ABOVE: The Calanche in the Scandola Nature Reserve. Established in 1975 and now listed as a world heritage site, the Scandola Nature Reserve is famed for its sheer red cliffs, some of which are 3,000 feet high, and inaccessible coves.

RIGHT: Situated northwest of Sartene is Filitosa, Corsica's leading prehistoric site. Megaliths and prehistoric carvings were discovered here in 1946. Surrounded by olive trees—some of which are over a thousand years old—these ancient monuments are thought to date as far back as the Neolithic era.

BELOW: The stunning gulf of Porto in the north of Corsica at sunset. The clear blue waters and profusion of sea life means that this area is one of the best for undersea diving.

LEFT: The narrow winding streets and alleyways in Bonifacio engender a genuine feeling of traveling back in time. The medieval quality of the town and its enclosing citadel makes this place the most visited in all Corsica.

ABOVE: Six miles off the southernmost point of Corsica lie the beguiling islands of Lavezzi. Formed from pink granite, these interesting configurations of rock also house a memorial to the many sailors who unfortunately lost their lives in the treacherous waters.

PAGE 346–347: Situated in the Regino Valley, the sprawling village of Speloncato is named after the nearby ravines (*e Spelunche* in Corsican). Overlooked by the massive Monte Grosso, the village has a beautiful market square, Romanesque church, and a bell tower dating from 1913.

BELOW: The citadel at Corte is the only one of Corsica's many citadels that was not built on the coast. This impressive edifice was built in 1419 by a Corsican aristocrat and then extended in the eighteenth and nineteenth centuries. The citadel now houses a museum devoted to Corsican culture and tradition.

ABOVE: The pretty town of Corbara in the
Balange region of Corsica boasts gorgeous views,
lush countryside, and a formerly Franciscan
monastery. Saint Dominic Convent was built in
1430 and still houses a spiritual center today.

PAGE 352–353: Parata Tower on the Sanguinaires Islands near Ajaccio is just one of the many remaining Genoese watchtowers that scatter the coastline of Corsica. The towers were originally built by the Genoese to act as an early-warning system against attacks from nearby Africa.

FRANCHE-COMTÉ

FRANCHE-COMTÉ

The area known as Franche-Comté did not officially exist until 1366. Previous to this date it had been a part of the mighty Burgundian empire. Through the course of its history, this tiny province has belonged to the Holy Roman Empire (1034), ceded to Austria (1481), owned by Spain (1556), and occupied by the French (1668). It was not until 1678 that is was officially recognized as part of France.

Franche-Comté is composed of the départements of Jura, Doubs, Haute-Saône, and the tiny Terretoire de Belfort (France's fifth smallest département).

One of the least-discovered parts of France, the Jura Mountains follow the Swiss border for 225 miles. The area is known for its "vin jaune" or yellow wine, hard aromatic cheeses, and cured sausages (known locally as Jesus sausages). The mountains offer some of the most challenging ski runs in France and each year a grueling cross-country ski race takes place here.

The capital of the region is Besançon. Famed for its clock-making industry during the eighteenth and nineteenth centuries, it has always been a home to pioneering spirits. The Lumière brothers, two of the very first film makers, were born here, as well as Victor Hugo, the author of *Les Miserables*).

Not far from Besançon is the city of Dole, the capital of Jura until 1479. The world-famous scientist, Louis Pasteur, was born here in the nineteenth century. His revolutionary works gave the world pasteurization and the first vaccine against rabies.

The small Terretoire de Belfort only became part of Franche-Comté in 1921; it had previously been part of Alsace. Apart from the extraordinary citadel and the

towering lion sculpture, it is best known these days for being the maker of TGV trains—France's *train grand vitesse* express train. It also hosts an annual rock festival—Les Eurockéennes—which rivals the annual Glastonbury, England event in size and spectacle.

The wine capital, Arbois, has its own Route du Vin where visitors can sample "vin jaune." This rich yellow nectar is allowed to mature for six years in oak casks which gives it its distinctive nutty flavor.

The breathtaking Haut-Jura Regional Park covers 300 square miles, starting from Chapelle-des-Bois and ending at the westernmost point of Lake Geneva. The grand Traversée du Jura is an arduous cross-country ski race following 130 miles of difficult paths; the highest of which is nearly 5,000 feet high and runs through one of the iciest valleys in France. Taking place each February, it is one of the largest races of its kind with an average of 4,000 skiers taking part.

PAGE 354–355: Chateau Chalon, perched on a hilltop, dominates Baume les Messieurs Valley. Not only is there a chateau and a twelfth-century abbey in this picturesque village, but it is also the home of the yellow wines that are made exclusively in this area.

LEFT: France has always excelled at civil engineering—here a railway viaduct.

ABOVE: The River Doub flows through a typical French village. The steep hills and climbing streets of the village, Lods, are fairly typical to all tiny hamlets in this locale.

PAGE 358–359: Bonlieu Lake is barely visible through the surrounding dense forests and can only be fully viewed from a nearby rocky outcrop. Such tranquillity makes it an ideal spot for fishing.

LEFT: A fifteenth-century carved gallery in Besançon, the capital of the Franche-Comté region. The city has kept much of its medieval charm, yet remains a vibrant youthful place, thanks to the many students housed here. This is one of the most popular places to live—the Battant quarter: traditionally a residential area for local wine makers, this area has kept many historic buildings.

ABOVE: The Château de Joux in La Cluse-et-Mijoux is only approachable through its enormous drawbridge. Built originally from wood in the eleventh century, then rebuilt in stone in the twelfth century by the Lords of Joux, it has been a fort, a prison, and more recently a museum. It was the site of Heinrich von Kleist's incarceration (the German poet and novelist was arrested for being a spy).

PAGE 362–363: Designed by Claude-Nicholas Ledoux in the nineteenth century to be the model of an ideal city, the Saline Royal or Royal Saltworks, never realized its original intention. Now listed as a World Heritage Site, this beautiful building is a fine example of industrial age logistics.

ABOVE: Chateau Joux stands on a hilltop
overlooking the peaceful village of Cluse en
Mijoux. Thought to have been built by the
Knights Templar during the eleventh century, it
was later remodeled by Maréchal Joffre in 1877.

PAGE 366: The quiet and provincial town of Dole was the capital of the Comte region until Louis XI ordered the town to be destroyed in 1479. The Collegiate de Notre Dame has a soaring belfry that offers comprehensive views of the surrounding countryside. Along the bank of the towns canal is Rue Pasteur, the birthplace of the famed biologist Louis Pasteur; the town commemorates his many achievements with statues and monuments dedicated to the scientist.

PAGE 367: The huge sculpture "The Lion of Belfort" was designed by Frederic Bartholdi, the original architect for the Statue of Liberty. The statue was completed in 1880. Made from pink sandstone, it was erected to celebrate the fighting spirit of Belfort. During a siege by the Prussians that lasted for 103 days, 17,000 Belfort fighters stood strong against 40,000 Prussian soldiers and won.

PREVIOUS PAGES: The Parc Naturel Régional du Haut-Jura is an area of untamed beauty. The largest town in the park, St. Claude is a quiet, unassuming village but it does own the world's largest pipe. Visitors to St. Claude can view the twenty-five-foot tall pipe anytime as it is propped up against the local town hall—presumably there to be used by the world's tallest mayor.

LEFT: The River Ognon glides past many ancient yet picturesque towns and villages on its way through the Saône Valley.

PAGE 372–373: In the old mining town of Ronchamp is the Chapelle de Notre Dame du Haut. This modernist church was designed by the well-known French architect Le Corbusier. One of the twentieth century's masterpieces in design, Le Corbusier claimed that the sweeping line of the chapel's roof was inspired by a hermit crab.

LEFT: The vineyards in the Jura region turn a vibrant golden hue during fall. This part of France is celebrated for its light white wines that are unique to the area.

ABOVE: The citadel in Besançon was built for Louis XIV in the late seventeenth century. The citadel now houses three fascinating museums; the Musée Comtois specializes in local customs and history; Musée d'Histoire Naturelle concerns the natural environment; and Musée de la Resistance et de la Déportation is a sobering look at Nazism and the French Resistance organization.

RHÔNE-ALPES

RHÔNE-ALPES

The Rhône-Alpes encompasses the départements of Ain, Ardèche, Drôme, Isère, Savoie, Loire, Rhône, and Haute-Savoie along the eastern border of France. Within its boundaries are attractions unlike anywhere else, the awe-inspiring Mont Blanc—Europe's highest peak—the plunging gorges of the Ardèche, tranquil Lake Geneva and the sophisticated jewel that is Lyon—the capital.

Lyon itself has been around since pre-Roman times. It is France's second largest city and the undisputed gastronomic capital of the country. Food here is a religion and best sampled in one of the many "Bouchons," the classic Lyonnais bistro—small, friendly, and brimming with local specialities, all served in a family atmosphere that beats any five-star restaurant. Old Lyon (or Vieux Lyon) also offers a few surprises: the most amazing are the traboules. These secret passageways interconnect underneath the city, linking houses that are far from each other. In total there are 315 secret pathways joining 230 streets with a total length of thirty miles. A few traboules

date as far back as Roman times but most were constructed during the nineteenth century for the safe transportation of silk during wet weather. (Lyon had been one of the major silk producers since the mideighteenth century with forty percent of its work force employed as silk weavers.) These hidden walkways also proved invaluable to the French Resistance during World War II.

Just northwest of Lyon are the sweeping vineyards of the Beaujolais wine region. Celebrated for its extremely drinkable and fruity red wines, the best time to visit the area is on the third Wednesday night of November. This is the earliest possible time that French law allows the bottles of Beaujolais Nouveau to be opened—a mere six weeks after bottling. Known as the "libération" or "mise en pierce" (the opening), the grand occasion is commemorated with a large street party and free wine for all.

PAGE 376–377: The clear and tranquil waters of the Lac de Chesery in Chamonix, France's legendary ski and rock climbing center, reflect the image of the nearby mountain ranges.

BELOW: A farmer begins to collect his walnut harvest. The Rhône-Alpes is the largest producer of walnuts in France and supplies fifty-one percent of the total supply—on average France harvests over 25,000 tons of walnuts each year.

PAGE 380–381: Here, on the western bank of the Saône, lies Old Lyon, a picture-postcard area of the city still full of flamboyant sixteenth century houses on cobblestone streets. Standing on the hill behind the old town is the Basilica Notre Dame de Fourvière and the Tour Metallique, an Eiffel tower-like construction built in 1893.

LEFT: Known as the "Venice of Savoie," Annecy is the capital of Haut-Savoie. Originally the capital to the once great House of Savoy—the previous Kings of Italy—it was recaptured during the French Revolution only to be returned to Savoy in 1815. Eventually the House of Savoy fell and all their lands were annexed into France including this charming city.

ABOVE: One of the most relaxing—and needless to say the easiest—ways to enjoy the views across the mountains is by taking the long tour on a ski lift. Beats hiking any day.

BELOW: There have been people living in the French Alps since prehistoric times; later, Celtic and Gaulish tribes settled around the lakes and valley. Used by various warring sides as a stronghold against attack (including French resistance fighters in World War II), the Alps have nevertheless remained a site of untouched beauty. These days the delicate natural balance of wildlife is protected in many nature parks.

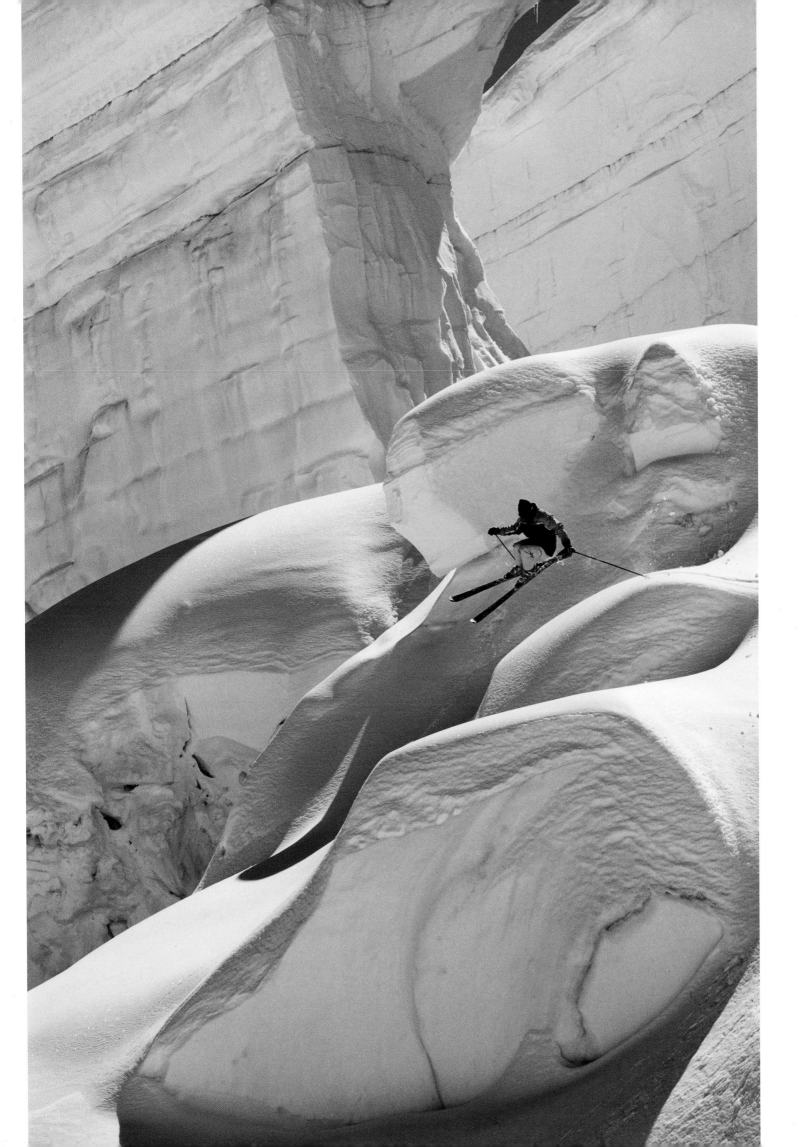

PAGE 388: The landscape of the French alps is estimated to be 44 million years old and the highest point is the majestic Mont Blanc, Europe's tallest mountain at 15,771 feet high.

PAGE 389: One of the most popular places for all winter sports, the Alps offers ski runs like nowhere else. Here a skier attempts to ride down the side of a glacier near the colossal Mont Blanc.

LEFT: The Beaujolais region, just northwest of Lyon, is known for its fruity red wines typically made from the Gamay grape. Vineyards stretch along the banks of the River Saône for thirty miles. The renowned Beaujolais Nouveau is enjoyed at a mere six weeks old.

PAGE 390–391: An alternative view of Annecy. Looking down the canals it is understandable how it has achieved the reputation as France's very own Venice.

ABOVE: A stonemason carves a statue of the
Madonna and Child on the roof of St. Nizier
Church in Lyon. The church was originally built
in the fourteenth and fifteenth centuries as a
monument to the early Christian martyrs of Lyon.
Additions to the church have been made
throughout the following years.

RIGHT: Standing high on a hillside, looking out
over Lyon, an angel stands guard.

PREVIOUS PAGES: The "Palais Idéal" was created by Ferdinand Cheval, a postman who used to walk twenty miles on foot every day to deliver his mail. One day he had a vision of a wonderful palace and spent the next thirty years collecting any interesting stones along his route and single-handedly shaping them into a building of incredible imagination and artistry.

ABOVE: Lyon contains a large Muslim community and one of the largest mosques in all of France. Here is the tall minaret of the celebrated building.

RIGHT: The Cathédrale St.-Jean in Lyon is a Gothic masterpiece. Work on the cathedral began in 1175 but took three centuries to complete. The building itself is striking but the most astounding detail is the astronomical clock situated on the northern side. This amazing feat of engineering can calculate all the feast days up to the year 2019 and work out the position of the stars over Lyon. When it chimes a cock crows, Angel Gabriel appears before Mary, and angels begin to sing.

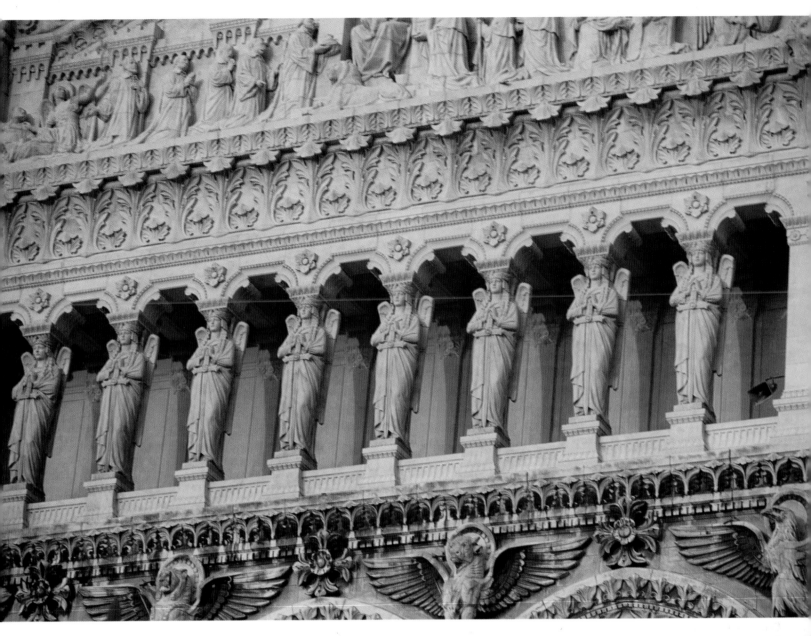

ABOVE: Crowning the hill behind Old Lyon is the
Basilica Notre Dame de Fourvière. Built in the
nineteenth century, it is highly decorated with
sculptures covering almost every square inch.

RIGHT: Cable cars carry passengers over the River
Isère into the hills above the St. Laurent Quarter
in the city of Grenoble. Situated in a valley
surrounded by snow covered mountains, Grenoble
enjoys a reputation for innovation, especially in
the fields of nuclear and microelectronics.

INDEX

Photo Credits